Problem
Seeking

Problem Seeking

An Architectural Programming Primer

By **William Peña**

With Steven Parshall

And Kevin Kelly

THIRD EDITION

AIA PRESS

Washington

International Standard Book Number: 0-913962-87-2

Printed in the United States of America.

AIA PRESS
1735 NEW YORK AVENUE, N.W.
WASHINGTON, D.C. 20006

Foreword

The first edition of *Problem Seeking* was directed to our clients, to business and facilities planning officials on the staffs of institutions, corporations and various public bodies. This was because our client's participation is so critical to the success of our projects. However, that first little booklet was discovered by practicing architects and architectural students. It was used in 1973 by the National Council of Architectural Registration Boards as a basis for the pre-design part of their new professional exam.

The second edition, then, was written for our clients, as well as architects and students. It joined a long shelf of books on architectural programming and the problem seeking method joined a long list of programming methods.

This third edition is a major revision, but the reader should be reassured that the theory behind the problem seeking method remains intact, having been tested through years of practice. This method still depends heavily on client participation and decision making.

As traditional architectural services expand to include pre-design programming at the beginning and building evaluation services at the end, the client's role becomes more and more vital in reaching decisions on which sound design solutions can be based and which will be tested after the building is occupied.

Many of the principles and techniques presented in this book can be attributed to Bill Caudill, one of the founders of CRSS, and ultimately an AIA Gold Medalist. Still other principles and techniques have evolved over a long period of architectural practice. They are not the product of one man, but the accumulated efforts of many members of the firm.

Tom Bullock
Chairman, CRSS Inc.

Contents

Part One

An Architectural Programming Primer

Part Two

The Appendix

Preface

CRSS was a pioneer in architectural programming. The first programming report dated 1950 by Bill Caudill illustrates many of the techniques, procedures, and principles included in this book. His article on "Architectural Analysis" in 1959 elicited a publisher's request to write a book on architectural programming. In 1969 Caudill encouraged John Focke and me to write the first PROBLEM SEEKING based on our experience as practicing programmers. The little booklet far exceeded the reception we anticipated. The material was well received by professionals in various disciplines who were predisposed toward organized methods of inquiry. Yet others found the material too esoteric and asked for a "popularized" version. Caudill responded with the idea for a small elementary book based on a slide presentation ... a primer to teach programming. PROBLEM SEEKING II was published in 1977.

And now, after nearly 10 years, PROBLEM SEEKING III is published as a major revision—not so much of the theory, but of the practical aspects affected by time, such as costs and expanded concepts and techniques. This time, Parshall and Kelly replace Caudill and Focke as co-authors. Updating cost figures would seem to be a useless exercise were it not for the importance of a balanced budget, and of quality levels as a means of matching a client's expectations with realistic price tags.

After 10 years of dipping into the information index for appropriate concepts, those recurring most often have been expanded from the original 12 to 24. Concepts are at the heart of programming because they tell us, in a common language, how the client wants to operate. And in an effort to improve the "how to do it" aspects of the book, we have introduced a typical programming schedule which features the squatters technique in more detail than before. These standard procedures are necessary for efficient teamwork.

This is again a two-part book: Part One is a primer on programming. Part Two is the appendix—a collection of supplemental material which would have complicated the primer. Whether you are an architect, a student or a client getting ready to start a building project, we have tried here to help you understand one programming method.

Architectural practice is an art as well as a science. As artists, we architects are under social pressure to be creative. We are tempted to create a different method for every new project. We love diversity, both in process and in product. And we are encouraged by the fact that any method can be made to work—at least once. As scientists, we are also under pressure to be creative, but in a more disciplined, more organized way. A scientific method is a systematic pursuit of knowledge. Programming is best as a systematic search for information.

The process described in this book is based on architectural practice—specifically designed to precede master planning and schematic design. The process, with slight changes in content, has been used to provide a broad spectrum of analyses leading to client decision-making and problem definition in interior design, engineering, construction and management services. These related analyses are not covered in this book in order to retain the elementary nature of this primer.

Some of our architect friends tell us we have done nothing more than document our experience as a method. Partly true. They relate to the process very well because we have experiences in common. Others tell us we've done nothing more than add the idea of concepts to the traditional problem solving method. Again partly true. Without concepts, a method leads inevitably to formalistic design. Actually, we developed this programming method by looking back at our experience and forward to the generalization of an organized framework which could be used repeatedly. It has worked successfully for us on over 1400 projects for more than 20 years. We know it can work for you.

Here then, is our revised third edition of PROBLEM SEEKING—An Architectural Programming Primer.

William Peña, FAIA
Founder, CRSS, Inc.
Houston, Texas 1987

Part One
An Architectural Programming Primer

The Primer

Good buildings don't just happen. They are planned to look good and perform well, and come about when good architects and good clients join in thoughtful, cooperative effort. Programming the requirements of a proposed building is the architect's first task, often the most important.

There are a few underlying principles that apply to programming—whether the most complex hospital or a simple house. This book concerns these principles.

Programming concerns five steps:

1 Establish **Goals.**

2 Collect and analyze **Facts.**

3 Uncover and test **Concepts.**

4 Determine **Needs.**

5 State the **Problem.**

The approach is at once simple and comprehensive—simple enough for the process to be repeatable for different building types and comprehensive enough to cover the wide range of factors which influence the design of buildings.

The five-step process applies to most any discipline—banking, engineering, or education, but when applied specifically to architecture, it needs its proper content. "Content" concerns the principle relating to an architectural product...a room, a building or a town. The principle is that a product has a much better chance of being successful if, during the design, the four major considerations are regarded simultaneously.

These considerations (or design determinants) indicate the types of information needed:

Function   Form   Economy   Time

Programming, therefore, involves an organized method of inquiry . . . a five-step process . . . interacting with four considerations.

The Search

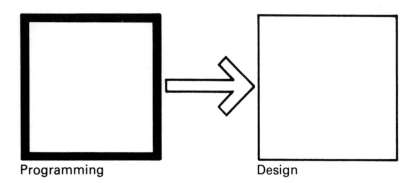

Programming   Design

Programming is a process. What kind? Webster spells it out specifically: "A process leading to the statement of an architectural problem and the requirements to be met in offering a solution."

This process, derived from the definition (referred to as the five-step process), is basic. The word "basic" is used advisedly. Since the advent of systematic programming two decades ago, different levels of sophistication have evolved. But the procedures presented here remain basic to all.

Back to the definition. Note "statement of an architectural problem." This implies problem solving. Although usually identified with scientific methods, problem solving is a creative effort. There are many different problem solving methods, but only those few which emphasize goals and concepts (ends and means) can be applied to architectural design problems.

Almost all of the methods include a step for problem definition—stating the problem. But most of the methods lead to confusing duality—finding out what the problem is and trying to solve it at the same time. You can't solve a problem unless you know what it is.

What, then, is the main idea behind programming? It's the search for sufficient information to clarify, to understand, to state the problem.

If programming is problem seeking, then design is problem solving.

These are two distinct processes, requiring different attitudes, even different capabilities. Problem solving is a valid approach to design if indeed the design solution responds to the client's design problem. Only after a thorough search for pertinent information can the client's design problem be defined or stated. "Seek and you shall define!"

Programmers and Designers

Who does what? Do designers program? They can, but it takes highly trained architects who are specialized in asking the right questions at the right time, who can separate wants from needs, and who have the skills to sort things out. Programmers must be objective (to a degree) and analytical, at ease with abstract ideas, and able to evaluate information and identify important factors while postponing irrelevant material. Designers can't always do this.

Designers generally are subjective, intuitive, and facile with physical concepts. Qualifications of programmers and designers are different.

Programmers and designers are separate specialists because the problems of each are very complex and require two different mental capabilities, one for analysis, another for synthesis.

It may well be that one person can manage both analysis and synthesis. If so, he* must be of two minds and use them alternately. However, for clarity, these different qualifications will be represented by different people — programmers and designers.

*Or she, as the case may be.

Analysis and Synthesis

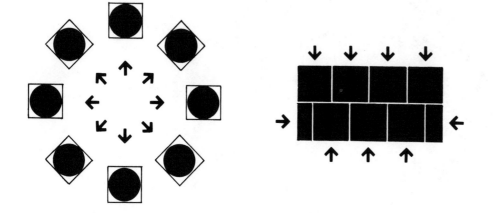

The total design process includes two stages: analysis and synthesis. In analysis the parts of a design problem are separated and identified. In synthesis the parts are put together to form a coherent design solution. The difference between programming and design is the difference between analysis and synthesis.

Programming IS analysis. Design IS synthesis.

You may not perceive the design process in terms of analysis and synthesis. You may even question problem solving as an approach. You may think of the design process as a creative effort. It is. But the creative effort includes similar stages: analysis becomes preparation or exposure and synthesis becomes illumination or insight. The total design process is, indeed, a creative process.

Does programming inhibit creativity? Definitely not! Programming establishes the considerations, the limits and possibilities of the design problem. (We prefer "considerations" to "constraints" to avoid being petulant.) Creativity thrives when the limits of a problem are known.

The Separation

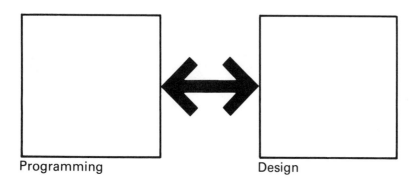

Programming   Design

Programming precedes design just as analysis precedes synthesis. The separation of the two is imperative, and avoids trial-and-error design alternatives. Separation is central to an understanding of a rational architectural process, which leads to good buildings.

This problem seeking method requires **a distinct separation of programming and design**.

Most designers love to draw, to make "thumbnail sketches," as they used to call them. Today the jargon is "conceptual sketches" and "schematics." Call them what you will, they can be serious deterrents in the planning of a successful building if done at the wrong time—before programming or during the programming process. Before the whole problem is defined, solutions can only be partial and premature. A designer, who cannot wait for a complete, carefully prepared program, is not unlike the tailor who doesn't bother to measure a customer before he starts cutting the cloth.

The experienced, creative designer withholds judgment, resists pre-conceived solutions and the pressure to synthesize, until all the information is in. He refuses to make sketches until he knows the client's problem. He believes in thorough analysis before synthesis. He knows that programming is the prelude to good design — although it does not guarantee it.

The Interface

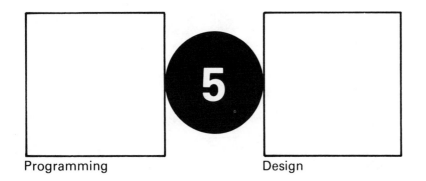

Programming   Design

The product of programming is the statement of the problem. The statement of the problem is the last step in problem seeking (programming), and it is also the first step in problem solving (design). **This problem statement, then, is the interface between programming and design.** It's the baton in a relay race. It's the hand-off from programmer to designer. In any case, the problem statement is one of the most important documents in the entire chain of the total project delivery system.

While many theorists extol the virtues of the statement of the problem, few practitioners stop to formulate it, to verbalize it. This programming method requires that you actually write out a clear statement of the problem. Since this statement is the first step in design as well as the last step in programming, its composition must be the joint effort of the designer and the programmer.

Five Steps

1 2 3 4 **5**

The competent programmer always keeps in mind the steps in programming: **(1) Establish Goals, (2) Collect Facts, (3) Uncover Concepts, (4) Determine Needs and (5) State the Problem.** The first three steps are primarily the search for pertinent information. The fourth is a feasibility test. The last step is distilling what has been found.

Curiously enough, the steps are alternately qualitative and quantitative. Goals, concepts and the problem statement are essentially qualitative. Facts and needs are essentially quantitative, for which the computer can be used.

Programming is based on a combination of interviews and work sessions. Interviews are used for asking questions and collecting data—particularly during the first three steps. Work sessions are used to verify information and to stimulate client decisions—particularly during the fourth step.

Briefly the five steps pose these questions:

1 **Goals**—*What* does the client want to achieve and *Why?*

2 **Facts**—*What* is it all about?

3 **Concepts**—*How* does the client want to achieve the goals?

4 **Needs**—*How* much money, space and quality?

5 **Problem Statement**—*What* are the significant conditions and the general directions the design of the building should take?

Procedure

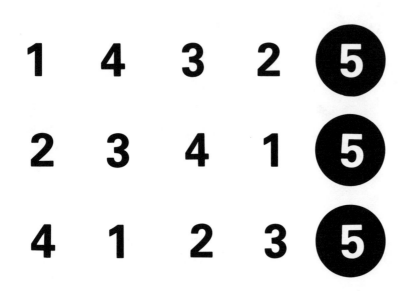

The five steps then are not inflexibly strict. They usually have no consistent sequence nor is the information scrupulously accurate. For example, a 10,000 student university, a 300-bed hospital, a 25-student classroom are only nominal, not actual sizes. The sources of information are not always reliable, and predictive capabilities may be limited.

The steps and the information then do not have the rigor nor accuracy of a mathematical problem. Programming, therefore, is a heuristic process and not an algorithm. As such, even good programming cannot guarantee finding the right problem, but it can reduce the amount of guesswork. The method is just as good as the judgment of the people involved.

Working through the steps in numerical sequence is preferable; theoretically, this is the logical order. But, in actual practice, **steps may be taken in a different order or at the same time** —all but the last step. It is frequently necessary, for example, to start with a given list of spaces and a budget (fourth step) before asking about Goals, Facts and Concepts (first, second and third steps). Most often it is necessary to work on the first four interacting steps simultaneously, cross-checking among these four steps for the integrity, the usefulness, the relevance and the congruence of information.

The fifth step is taken only after marshalling all the previous information, extracting, abstracting and getting to the very essence of the problem.

The Whole Problem

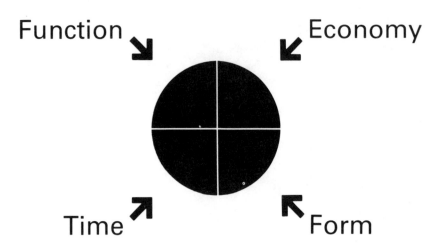

It's important to search and find the whole problem. It must be identified in the areas of **Function, Form, Economy, and Time.** Classify information accordingly. This simplifies the problem while maintaining a comprehensive approach. A wide range of factors makes up the whole problem, but all can be classified in the four areas which serve later as design considerations.

Too little information leads to a partial statement of the problem and a subsequent premature and partial design solution. The appropriate amount of information should be broad enough in scope to pertain to the whole design problem, but not so broad as to pertain to some universal problem. As the Spanish proverb states: "He who grasps too much, squeezes little." Grasp only what you can manage and what will be useful to the designer.

As a professor might say, "Before you answer individual questions, be sure to look at the whole examination." The designer should look at the whole problem before starting to solve any of its parts. If the designer does not have a clear understanding of the whole problem, how can he come up with a comprehensive solution?

Four Considerations

Function	1 people 2 activities 3 relationships
Form	4 site 5 environment 6 quality
Economy	7 initial budget 8 operating costs 9 life cycle costs
Time	10 past 11 present 12 future

Take a closer look at Function, Form, Economy and Time. **There are three key words to each consideration.**

Function implies "what's going to happen in their building." It concerns activities, relationship of spaces, and people—their number and characteristics. Key words are: (1) People, (2) Activities, (3) Relationships.

Form relates to the site, the physical environment (psychological, too) and the quality of space and construction. Form is what you will see and feel. It's the "what is there now" and "what will be there." Key words are: (4) Site, (5) Environment and (6) Quality.

Economy concerns the initial budget and quality of construction, but also may include consideration of operating and life cycle costs. Key words are: (7) Initial Budget, (8) Operating Costs, (9) Life Cycle Costs.

Time has three classifications—past, present and future—which deal with the influences of history, the inevitability of changes from the present and projections into the future. Key words are: (10) Past, (11) Present, (12) Future.

Framework

	1	2	3	4	5
Function					
Form					
Economy					
Time					

Use the four considerations to guide you at each step during programming. By establishing a systematic set of relationships between steps and considerations, between process and content, a comprehensive approach is assured. The interweaving of steps and considerations forms a framework for information covering the whole problem.

All four considerations interact at each step. For example, in the first step when goals are investigated, function goals, form goals, economy goals and time goals should emerge. With each of these having three sub-categories, then the process includes asking twelve pertinent questions regarding goals alone. Since the first three steps constitute the main search for information, three times twelve provides the basis for thirty-six pertinent questions.

Consider these as key questions. The answers will provide opportunities for further questions. The following Information Index indicates more than ninety items in these three steps.

Programmers do not have to know everything the client knows, but they should know enough of the client's aspirations, needs, conditions, and ideas that will influence the design of the building. For this, programmers have to know the right questions to ask; they start with the thirty-six sub-categories.

The considerations interact in the fourth step to test the economic feasibility of the project; and in the last step they interact to state the whole problem.

This interaction provides a framework to classify and document information. The classification qualities inherent in this framework are particularly useful in avoiding information clogs when dealing with massive quantities of information. The categories are broad enough to classify the many bits of information without nit-picking and indecision.

The framework can be used as a checklist for missing information. As such, the orderly display of information on a wall becomes a good visual scoreboard. One glance at a wall display of graphic analysis material can spot what is missing and needs to be documented. It also provides a format for dialogue among the members of the team.

Information Index

The framework can be extended to serve as an Information Index—**a matrix of key words to be used to seek out appropriate information.** These key words are specific enough to cover the scope of major factors, universal enough to be negotiable for different building types. Even if some key words are not seemingly applicable in a particular project, it is useful to test them—ask a question based on those key words. If the test proves them to be applicable, then those key words will encourage a thorough search for information. They may offer a better and quicker understanding of the project.

Most key words are "evocative words." They trigger useful information. Charged with emotion as well as meaning, they tend to evoke a response, or even to suggest likely substitutions.

An Information Index may be designed to be very specific

and tailored to one building type; but as all such check lists, it would soon be obsolete. A general character prolongs its usefulness.

Note that the Information Index establishes the interrelationship of information regarding Goals, Facts and Concepts. For example, a functional goal for "efficiency" is related to "space adequacy" and is implemented by effective "relationships"—reading horizontally on the index. Also note that items under Needs and Problem are more limited since the fourth step is a feasibility test and the last step is abstracting the essence of the project.

The following chart has been adapted from the **Architectural Registration Handbook, A Test Guide for Professional Exam Candidates,** published jointly by the National Council of Architectural Registration Boards and Architectural Record, 1973.

Information Index

	Goals	Facts
Function	Mission	Statistical data
People	Maximum number	Area parameters
	Individual identity	Manpower/workloads
	Interaction/privacy	User characteristics
	Ranking of values	Community characteristics
	Exercise of authority	Authority structure
Activities	Security	Value of potential loss
	Progression	Time-motion study
	Segregation	Traffic analysis
	Encounters	Behavioral patterns
	Efficiency	Space adequacy
Relationships	Information exchange	Type/intensity
Form	Bias on site elements	Site analysis
Site	Sound structure	Soil analysis
	Efficient land use	F.A.R. and G.A.C.
	Physical comfort	Climate analysis
	Life safety	Code survey
Environment	Sociality	Surroundings
	Individuality	Psychological implications
	Encoded direction	Point of reference
	Direct entry	Entry symbols
	Projected image	Generic nature
Quality	Building quality level	Cost/S.F.
	Spatial quality level	Building efficiency
	Technical quality level	Equipment costs
	Functional quality level	Area per unit
Economy	Extent of funds	Cost parameters
Initial Budget	Cost effectiveness	Maximum budget
	Maximum return	Time-use factors
	Return on investment	Market analysis
Operating Costs	Minimize operating costs	Energy source-costs
	Maintenance and operating costs	Activities and climate factors
Lifecycle Costs	Reduce life cycle costs	Economic data
Time	Historic preservation	Significance
Past	Static/dynamic activities	Space parameters
	Change	Activities
Present	Growth	Projections
	Occupancy date	Durations
Future	Cost controlled growth	Escalation factors

Concepts	Needs	Problem

Service grouping
People grouping
Activity grouping
Priority
Hierarchy
Security controls
Sequential flow
Separated flow
Mixed flow
Relationships
Communication
	Space requirements
	Parking requirements
	Outdoor space requirements
	
	Functional alternatives
		Unique and important
		  performance requirements
		  which will shape building
		  design

Enhancement
Special foundations
Density
Environmental controls
Safety precautions
Neighbors
Home base
Orientation
Accessibility
Character
Quality control
	Site development costs
	
	Environmental influences on costs
	
	Building cost/S.F.
	Building efficiency
	Equipment costs
		Major form considerations
		  which will affect building
		  design

Cost control
Efficient allocation
Multi-function
Merchandising
Energy conservation
Cost control
Cost control
	Cost estimate analysis
	
	Energy budget (if reqd)
	Operating costs (if reqd)
	Life cycle costs (if reqd)
		Attitude towards the initial
		  budget and its influence on the
		  fabric and geometry of the
		  building

Adaptability Tolerance Convertibility Expansibility Linear/concurrent scheduling Phasing	 Time schedule Time/cost schedule	Implications of change/growth on long-range performance

Organizing Information

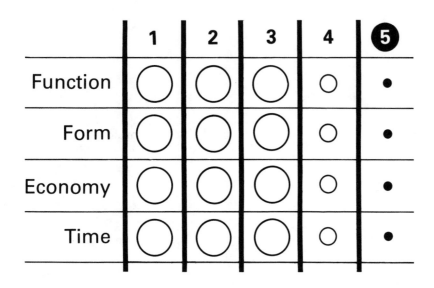

	1	2	3	4	5
Function	◯	◯	◯	○	•
Form	◯	◯	◯	○	•
Economy	◯	◯	◯	○	•
Time	◯	◯	◯	○	•

The programmer establishes order so that information can make sense and can be used effectively in discussions and decision making. **The programmer organizes and classifies information.** He extracts information and displays it. He stimulates decisions from client groups. He organizes the client's vast world of information with a rational framework. Without this framework, his verification with the client and his handoff to the designer would not be possible.

With this framework the programmer can classify the information, placing it into broad compartments. Since the main search for information is made in the first three steps, it can be expected that the largest quantities of information are found in those first compartments. Refer to the accompanying diagram. On the other hand, the space requirements and their economic feasibility represent a diminished amount of information in the fourth step. And, of course, the fifth step should represent the least amount of information, yet the most important.

The handoff package—the programming document including a clear, simple statement of the problem—must represent the epitome of organized, edited information free of irrelevance.

Two-Phase Process

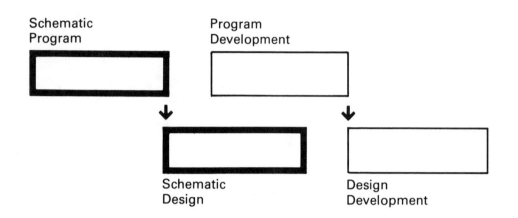

Schematic Program

Program Development

Schematic Design

Design Development

Schematic program and program development provide the information needed at the two successive design phases, going from the general scope to particular details. **Programming is a two-phase process related to the two phases of design**—schematic design and design development.

Schematic design depends on major concepts and needs which should not be lost in the mass of information unusable in this phase. Designers must have information that clarifies major design determinants—those factors which will shape the broad composition of the building. The schematic program must provide this important over-all information useful in schematic design.

However, equally as critical is the filtering out and the postponing of information which is not needed in schematic design. Give designers only the information they need at the time they need it.

Design development is what the words imply: the detailed development of schematic design. Program development provides the specific room details—furniture and equipment requirements, environmental criteria (atmospheric, visual and acoustic) and service requirements (mechanical and electrical). The second phase of programming may be in progress when the designer is doing schematic design.

It should be pointed out however, that the programmer, in dealing with unfamiliar and critical areas, must seek and collect specific details earlier than normally needed in order to establish adequate and generalized space requirements for schematic design.

Data Clog

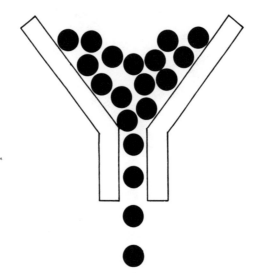

The amount of information received from a client can be staggering. Don't let the flood of information bother you. One trick is to determine when the information will be most useful—in schematic design or in design development. Any quantity of client-furnished information can be organized for use at the appropriate phase. A programmer needs experience and good judgment to know in which phase to use the information—even more experience and judgment to cull out trivial and irrelevant information to eliminate data clog.

Yes, people become data clogged with too much unorganized information—which causes confusion and prevents clear conclusions. Data clog paralyzes the thought processes, and a mental block against all information develops. Unable to comprehend it, a designer may decide to ignore it all, throw up his hands and say, "Don't bother me with all those facts. I know what I must do—I'll limit the information to what I already know."

One can assimilate any amount of information as long as it is pertinent, meaningful and well organized for effective use. Large amounts of highly organized material are required to expand the range of possibilities before a new and useful combination of ideas can be generated by the designer.

Processing and Discarding

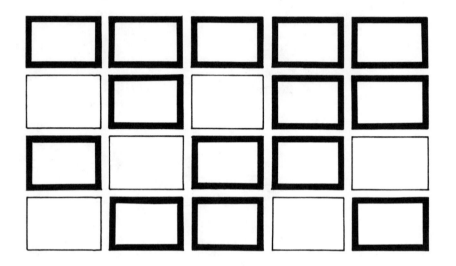

Programming concerns the processing of raw data into useful information. For example, course enrollments at a college are not useful information - until they can be manipulated mathematically with average class size, periods attended per week, total periods available for scheduling and classroom utilization. Only when the process produces the number and size of classrooms required does the raw data become useful information.

Raw data relating to climate analysis or soil analysis also becomes meaningful information only when architectural implications are determined. After that's accomplished the raw data can be discarded or placed in an appendix where it will not cause data clog.

To quote an old saying, "Any fool can add, it takes a genius to subtract." It takes a "genius" to discard information as being irrelevant to a design problem or merely too trivial to affect the design one way or another. Although programming is primarily conscious analysis, intuition has its place—**the sensitivity to know what information will be useful and what should be discarded.** The risk in discarding useful information is minimized with experience.

Abstract To The Essence

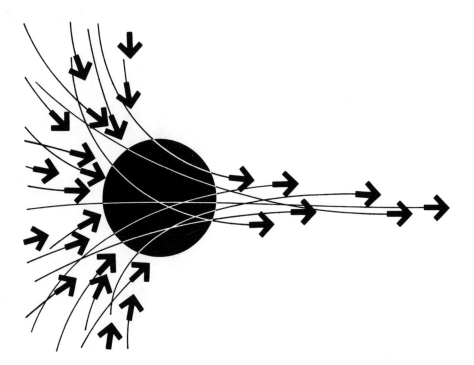

Architects are taught to take a holistic view of the problem, and even to go beyond the sphere of direct influences to explore other possibilities. However, going too far afield increases the prospects of irrelevant information.

Architects are also taught to bring order out of chaos, to establish an order of importance, to get to the heart of the matter. Abstracting—distilling—to the essence, must be an essential talent of the programmer. **There must be a filtering process which brings out only the major aspects of information**. This is especially true in arriving at the statement of the problem.

There is always the danger of oversimplification in abstracting to find the essence. Yet the danger of leaving something out can be minimized by analyzing and consciously including all the complicating factors.

There is need to amplify, to view the whole problem; but there is also need to abstract. You amplify and then narrow down; you seek the ramifications of the information gathered; then you turn around to determine the bare implications. It's a continual process. You must be able to see the trees *and* the forest—not both at once but consecutively, from two different points of view.

User On Team

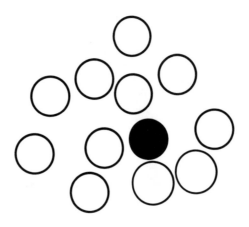

The user is an expert in the use of the building. He may assume that he knows what he wants better than anyone else. He may be right. Or he may ask the architect or a consultant to find out what he needs. **The user must be a contributing member of the project team.**

Dealing with the user calls for different strategies to determine reasonable requirements; nevertheless, the building should benefit by intensive user participation in the programming process.

Users are sometimes suspicious that a building will represent only the self expression of the architect. This concerns the familiar argument involving form and function.

On the other hand, the architect is sometimes suspicious that the user is being ideosyncratic in his requirements and that no one else can use the building without major remodeling.

Usually, architects love to design buildings tailor-made to specific user requirements which provide opportunities for novel designs. This is particularly true of tailored residences—where the owner/user is directly responsible for the outcome.

Organizations and institutions with static or dynamic conditions bring up the issue of ideosyncratic versus negotiable requirements. But remember, the user's first concern is how his needs will be met when the building is occupied.

Team

Programming requires team effort. **The project team should be led by two responsible group leaders**—one to represent the client and the other to represent the architect. They must work together toward a successful project. Each leader must be able to:

- Coordinate the individual efforts of his group members.

- Make decisions or cause them to be made.

- Establish and maintain communication within, and between, the two groups.

The project team must have good management.

Many people participate in programming a project. There is the traditional participation of the client/owner and the client/manager. More and more the client/users and the client/spectators (community people) are becoming active in programming. This means that the approach to programming should be rational enough to withstand public scrutiny and analytical enough to achieve a greater mutual understanding of the issues.

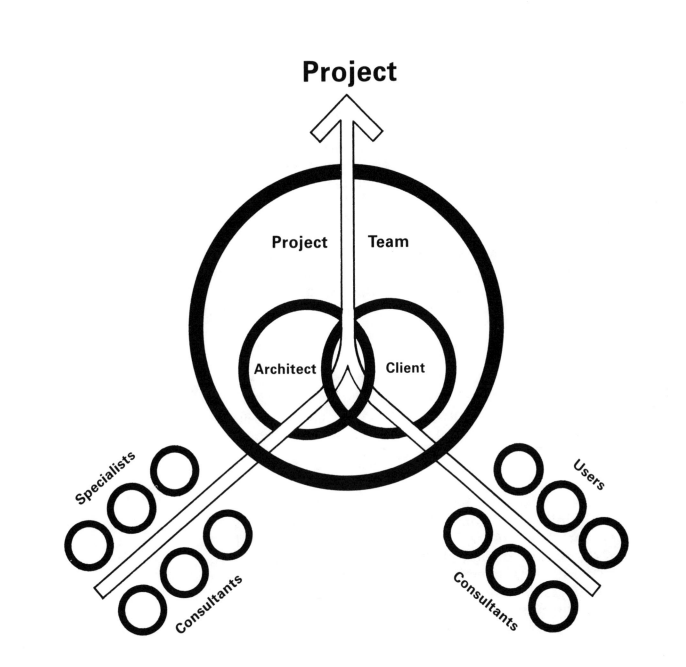

The increased involvement generates much more data. This increased involvement also causes more conflicting information. The users are concerned with the hope for greater satisfaction of their needs; the owner is concerned with cost reduction and cost control. Exposure of the owner's and users' differences is the first step in reconciliation. Conflicts are often reconciled by the introduction of human values not previously considered by the owner.

Participants on the team must communicate and be willing to cooperate with one another. This precludes the prima donna client or the prima donna architect who competes to play every role on the team, so as to make every decision in programming and in design.

The client has the major responsibility to be creative in programming for he is the one responsible for the operational outcome. The programmer can act as a catalyst in seeking new combinations of ideas. He can test new ideas and spawn alternatives.

The designer must be creative in the design phase for he is responsible for the physical and psychological environment. The programmer must keep the client from making premature design decisions during programming. He should raise the client's appreciation and aspiration for better buildings. In short, the programmer should prepare for the designer the best possible environment for creativity.

Background Information

Although the five-step process is the same for any building type, **there may necessarily be a preparatory step.** This will depend on the experience (or inexperience) that the programmer brings to the project. For example, if the project were a school, and the programmer had no experience in programming schools, then he must develop a background understanding of schools. He should visit similar schools; do library research; and talk to educators and consultants. He needs to understand the jargon of the client and the general nature of the building type.

The programmer starts with an analytical attitude. He approaches the project in an organized manner. His background and experience relate to the specific type of building. If not, the preparatory step is required.

With proper background information, the programmer helps the client to determine the number and kinds of consultants and when they might be most effectively brought into the total design process.

Decision Making

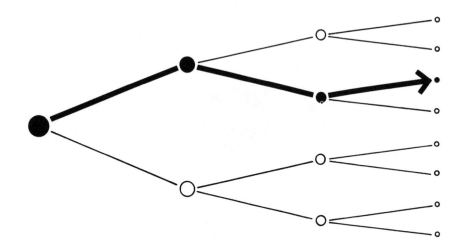

Good programming is characterized by timely and sound decision making by the client—not the programmer. During programming the client decides what he wants to accomplish and how he wants to do it. The programmer may have to evaluate the gains and risks in order to stimulate a decision. He must identify for the client those decisions that need to be made prior to design.

Although complete objectivity is not required, the programmer must emphasize the client's decisions and not his own; and his questions should not be based on a preconceived solution. He may stimulate client decisions by spawning options and by testing programmatic concepts. He may ask, for example, "Have centralized kitchen services been considered as opposed to several decentralized kitchens?" Goals and concepts must be displayed so that decision makers can understand alternative concepts and evaluate their effect on goals.

The programmer must stimulate client decisions. This avoids having to reprogram after the designer is at work. When the client's decisions lead to a well-stated problem, any needed recycling back from design to programming is a minor activity and will not seriously affect the design solution.

When a client postpones decisions, the design solutions tend to be unfeasible. If the client cannot decide on how much money to spend on the project until he sees the design, the inevitable will happen. The design solution will exceed the extent of funds available.

Decisions made during programming eliminate the expense of numerous design alternatives. If merely two design alternatives are made for each indecision, the number of alternatives increases expotentially. Indecision then, increases the complexity of the design problem, definitely to be avoided. On the other hand, **every decision the client makes during programming simplifies the design problem** by reducing the number of alternative design solutions to those which meet the program requirements. Organizational and functional decisions produce clear requirements which lead to limited design alternatives, highly desirable.

While emphasis is placed on client decision making, it must be realized that this authority is often vested on other people and agencies. Understanding who will actually make which decisions is crucial. The Chief Administrator? The administrators of funding and the code agencies? Generally, he who has the responsibility for the outcome has the authority to make the decisions. Interview *him!* Then insist on his approval of the program.

Communication

To achieve effective, clear communication among many people—professionals, clients, users—information collected must be carefully documented. Undocumented information is not likely to be considered and evaluated by the client and the designer. The programmer collects, organizes and displays the information for discussion, evaluation and consensus. **Team effort demands communication**.

Clients and designers require graphic analysis in order to fully comprehend the magnitude of numbers and the implication of ideas. This means there is a need to use communication techniques (brown sheets, analysis cards, gaming cards) to promote thorough understanding which leads to sound decision making.

A flow-chart diagram is comprehended more quickly than a written description. Use graphic images which are simple and include only one thought at a time. Keep the images specific enough to clarify the thought, but general and abstract enough to evoke a range of design possibilities. These should help client understanding and cater to the designer's thinking and drawing skills.

Establish GOALS

Goals are important to the designer who wants to know the what and why of things—more than a list of spaces. He'll not find inspiration in a list. He will in goals. **Project goals indicate what the client wants to achieve, and why.**

However goals must be tested for integrity, for usefulness and for relevance to the architectural design problem. To test them it is necessary to understand the practical relationship between goals and concepts.

If goals indicate what the client wants to achieve, concepts indicate how the client wants to achieve them. In other words, goals are implemented through concepts.

Goals are the ends. Concepts, the means. Concepts are ways of achieving goals. The relationship of goals and concepts is one of congruence. The test for the integrity of goals depends on their congruence with concepts.

Practical goals have concepts to implement them. Lip-service goals, on the other hand, have no integrity and should be disregarded. They may well be faithless promises in a public relations publication with no plan to keep them. Regardless of good intentions, it is not always what the client says but what he really means.

No one can argue against "motherhood" goals. They are unassailable; however, they are too general to be directly useful. Who can argue against the goal "to provide a good environment?" Or "to get the most for the money?" There's nothing wrong with including a few "motherhood" goals, especially if they can be processed to be specific enough to clarify the situation; however intellectually hard, clear project goals are absolutely essential.

On the other hand a few "motherhood" goals are needed to inspire designers, who like ambiguity to trigger the subconscious in their search for design concepts.

Do not forget that trying to mix problems and solutions of different kinds causes never-ending confusion. To put it positively, a social problem calls for a social solution. After there is a social solution then it can be part of a design problem for which there will be a design solution. You cannot solve a social problem with an architectural solution.

Goals and concepts must be tested for pertinence to a design problem and not to a social or some other related problem. This test for relevance includes testing goals and concepts for design implications that might qualify them as part of a design problem.

Collect and Analyze FACTS

Facts are only important if they are appropriate. Facts are used to describe the existing conditions of the site including the physical, legal, climatic and aesthetic aspects. These facts about the site should be documented graphically to be really effective. Other important facts include statistical projections, economic data and descriptions of the user characteristics. There's no end to facts. **Yet programming must be more than fact finding.**

The facts (and figures) can become too numerous to promote definite conclusions. Collect only those that might have a bearing on the problem and organize them into categories. Seek facts that are pertinent to the goals and concepts. Massage these facts and figures to become useful information. Process them to determine the architectural implications.

Facts may involve many numbers—such as the number of

people which generates space requirements: 2000 seats in a concert hall. Numbers need to be accurate enough to insure the impartial allocation of space and money, yet rounded out enough to allow for a loose fit: 150 square feet per office occupant. Predictive parameters have to be just accurate enough to be realistic: 15 square feet per dining seat.

When a programmer asks questions, what he hears may not be what he wants to hear; nevertheless, he must try to avoid a bias so as to collect impartial information. He must avoid preconceptions and face the facts squarely. He must be realistic, neither optimistic nor pessimistic. He must separate fact from fantasy. He must seek what is true or even what is assumed to be true. Assumptions in this case are things to be lived with. He must tell the difference between established fact and mere opinion. He must evaluate opinions and test their validity.

Uncover and Test CONCEPTS

It is critical to **understand the difference between programmatic concepts and design concepts,** very difficult for some people to grasp.

Programmatic concepts refer to abstract ideas intended mainly as functional solutions to clients' performance problems without regard to the physical response. On the other hand, design concepts refer to concrete ideas intended as physical solutions to clients' architectural problems, this being the physical response. The key to comprehension is that programmatic concepts relate to performance problems and design concepts relate to architectural problems.

The difference between programmatic concepts and design concepts is illustrated in these examples: *convertibility* is a programmatic concept; a corresponding design concept is a *folding door. Shelter* is a programmatic concept; a corresponding design concept is a *roof.*

Abstract ideas are required. Ideas must be kept in a pliable, vague form until the designer jells them into a physical solution. It's really best if design can wait until all the information is available. Should the client prescribe independent concrete ideas or three-dimensional design concepts, the designer would have difficulty in articulating solid-form solutions into an integrated whole.

Such is the case when a house client drops a big scrapbook on your desk full of magazine clippings representing a parade of actual design solutions—a Dutch kitchen, a French Provincial dining room, a Japanese living room, together with a Shangri-la porch. The scrapbook is the nemesis of the experienced programmer; yet it can be used as a means to seek the problems behind the solutions.

There are twenty-four programmatic concepts that seem to crop up on nearly every project, regardless of the building types—housing, hospitals, schools, shopping centers, or factories. The next series of diagrams explains briefly these recurring concepts. The programmer will find them useful by testing to see if they are applicable to his current project.

1. Priority

2. Hierarchy

The concept of priority evokes questions regarding **the order of importance,** such as relative position, size and social value. This concept reflects how a goal based on a **ranking of values** is to be accomplished. For example, "To place a higher value on pedestrian traffic than on vehicular traffic" may relate to the precedence in traffic flow.

The concept of hierarchy is related to a goal about the exercise of authority and is expressed in **symbols of authority.** For example, the goal "to maintain the traditional hierarchy of military rank" may be implemented by the concept of a hierarchy of office sizes.

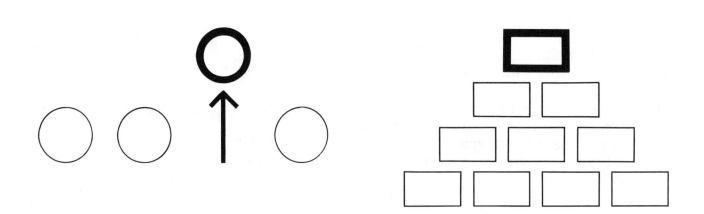

3. Character

The concept of character is based on a goal concerning **the image** the client wants to project in terms of values and the generic nature of the project.

4. Density

A goal for efficient land or space use or a goal to respond to harsh climatic conditions may lead to the appropriate degree of density–**low, medium or high density.**

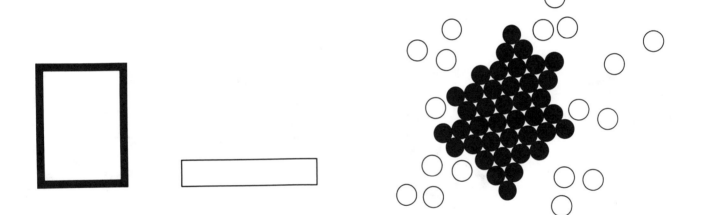

5. Service Grouping

6. Activity Grouping

Should services be **centralized** or **decentralized?** Test the many services as being best centralized or best decentralized. Should the heating system be centralized or decentralized? The library? And dining? And storage? And many other services? Evaluate the gains and risks to simulate client decisions. But remember each distinct service will be centralized or decentralized for a definite reason—to implement a specific goal.

Should activities be **integrated** or **compartmentalized?** A family of closely related activities would indicate integration to promote interaction, while the need for some kinds and degrees of privacy would indicate compartmentalization.

7. People Grouping

Look for concepts derived from the physical, social and emotional characteristics of people—**as individuals, in small groups, in large groups.** If a client wants to preserve the identity of individuals in large masses of people, ask what size grouping would implement this goal. Look to the functional organization and not to the organizational chart which merely indicates pecking order.

8. Home Base

Home base is related to the idea of **territoriality**—an easily defined place where a person can maintain his or her individuality.

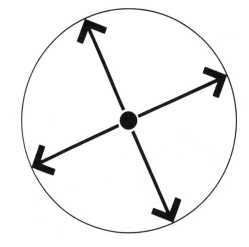

9. Relationships

The correct interrelation of spaces promotes efficiencies and effectiveness of people and their activities. This concept of **functional affinities** is the most common concept.

10. Communications

A goal to promote the effective exchange of information or ideas in an organization may call for **networks or patterns** of communication: Who communicates with whom? How? How often?

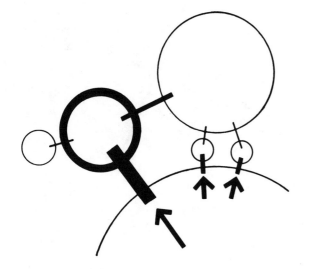

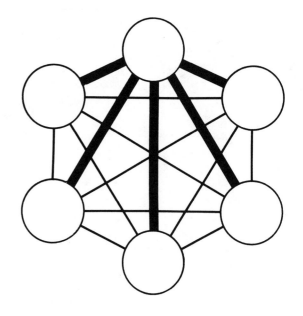

11. Neighbors

Is there a goal for sociality? Will the project be completely **independent** or is there a mutual desire to be **interdependent,** to cooperate with neighbors?

12. Accessibility

Can first-time visitors find where to enter the project? The concept of accessibility also applies to provisions for the handicapped beyond **signs and symbols.** Single or multiple entrances?

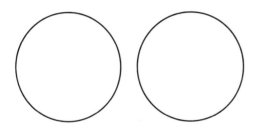

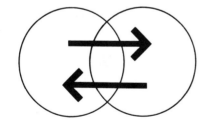

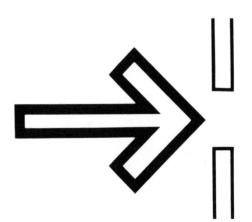

13. Separated Flow

A goal for segregation may relate to people (such as prisoners and public), to automobiles, (such as campus traffic and urban traffic) and to people and automobiles (such as pedestrian traffic and automobile traffic). **Separate traffic lanes with barriers** such as walls, separate floors, and space.

14. Mixed Flow

Common social spaces, such as town squares or building lobbies, are designed for **multi-directional, multi-purpose traffic**–or mixed flow. This concept may be apropos if the goal is to promote chance and planned encounters.

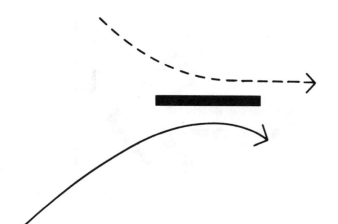

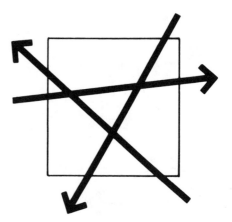

15.   Sequential Flow

16.   Orientation

The progression of people (as in a museum) **and things** (as in a factory) must be carefully planned. A flow-chart diagram will communicate this concept of sequential flow much easier than words.

Provide a bearing—a **point of reference** within a building, a campus, or a city. Relating periodically to this space, thing, or structure can prevent a feeling of being lost.

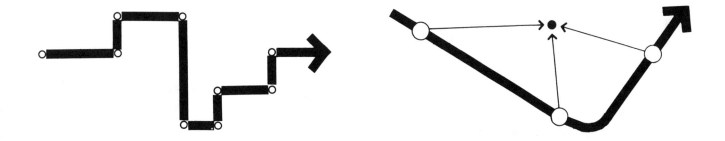

17. Flexibility

18. Tolerance

The concept of flexibility is quite often misunderstood. To some it means that the building can accommodate growth through expansion. To others it means that the building can allow for changes in function through the conversion of spaces. To still others it means that the building provides the most for the money through multi-function spaces. Actually flexibility covers all three—**expansibility, convertibility, versatility.**

This concept may well add space to the program. Is a particular space **tailored** precisely for a static activity or is it provided with a **loose fit** for a dynamic activity—one likely to change?

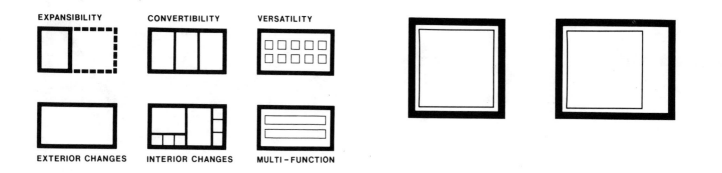

EXPANSIBILITY CONVERTIBILITY VERSATILITY

EXTERIOR CHANGES INTERIOR CHANGES MULTI-FUNCTION

19. Safety

Which major ideas will implement the goal for life safety? Look to **codes and safety precautions** for form-giving ideas.

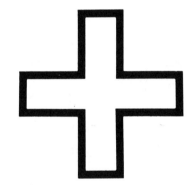

20. Security Controls

The degree of security control varies depending upon the value of the potential loss–**minimum, medium or maximum**. These controls are used to protect property and to control personnel movement.

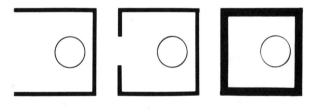

21. Energy Conservation

There are two general ways to lead to energy-efficient buildings: **(a) keep heated area to a minimum** by making use of conditioned, but non-heated, outside space such as exterior corridors; and **(b) keep heat-flow to a minimum** with insulation, correct orientation to sun and wind, compactness, sun controls, wind controls and reflective surfaces.

22. Environmental Controls

What controls for **air temperature, light and sound** will be required to provide for people comfort **inside and outside** the building? Look to the climate and sun angle analysis for answers.

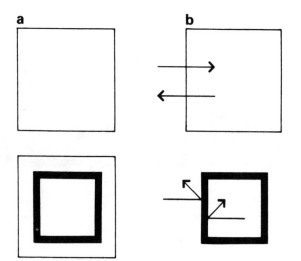

23. Phasing

24. Cost Control

Will phasing of construction be required to complete the project on a **time and cost** schedule if the project proved infeasible in the initial analysis? Will the urgency for the occupancy date determine the need for concurrent scheduling or allow for linear scheduling?

This concept is intended as a search for economy ideas which will lead to a **realistic preview of costs** and a balanced budget to meet the extent of available funds.

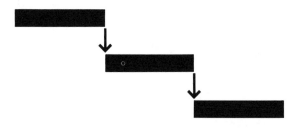

Determine NEEDS

Few clients have enough money to do all the things they want to do. Therefore, distinguishing *needs* from *wants* is important. What the rich man considers a necessity, the poor man thinks a luxury. Thus, judgments on the quality and adequacy of space are difficult to make. It is also difficult to identify real *needs.* The client usually wants more than he can afford. So the client and the architect must agree on a quality level of construction and on a definite space program relating to funds available at a specific time.

The fourth step is in effect an economic feasibility test to see if a budget can be determined, or a fixed budget balanced. It should be noted that the best balance is achieved when all four elements of cost are to some extent negotiable: (1) the space requirements, (2) the quality of construction, (3) the money budget, and (4) time. At least one of these four elements must be negotiable. Thus, if agreement is reached on quality, budget and time, the adjustment must be made in the amount of space. A serious imbalance might require the re-evaluation of Goals, Facts and Concepts.

The client's functional needs have a direct bearing on space requirements, which are generated by people and activities. Allowance must be made for a reasonable building efficiency as expressed by the relationship of net to gross areas.

The proposed quality of construction is expressed in quantitative terms as cost per square foot. A realistic escalation factor must be included to cover the time lag between programming and mid-construction.

Phasing of construction may be considered as an alternative:

When the initial budget is limited.

When the funds are available over a period of time.

When the functional needs are expected to grow.

Cost control begins with programming, and is basic to the whole architectural design problem to be solved.

Cost control does not inhibit an architect's creativity; Economy is a major consideration, not a constraint. An architect might petulantly think that cost control is a constraint, but not if he is committed to give the client what he needs, what he can afford.

Predicting costs at programming is not too difficult since the total planning proceeds from the general to the specific, from the broad scope to details. During programming, cost estimates can be made by successive approximations from the roughest tally of gross area, testing it with different quality levels of construction, while keeping an eye on building cost and other anticipated expenditures.

First phase programming (for schematic design) requires schematic estimates. Second phase programming (for design development) requires more detailed estimates. As the project advances in refinement, it is possible to test, to re-balance and up-date the budget.

Cost Estimate Analysis

It is imperative to establish a realistic budget from the very beginning. **Realistic budgets are predictive and comprehensive.** They avoid major suprises. They tend to include all the anticipated expenditures as line items in a cost estimate analysis. The architect must look to past experience and published material to derive predictive parameters.

The budget depends upon three realistic predictions: (1) a reasonable efficiency ratio of net to gross area, (2) cost per square foot escalated to mid-construction, (3) other expenditures as percentages of building cost. These predictions have become so common a practice that no one considers them as predictions but as planning factors.

What happens when a trial-run cost estimate analysis results in a total budget amount required (line K) larger than the extent of funds available? In other words, the client cannot afford the total cost. If the budget is fixed for a specific time, only two other factors can change: cost per square foot and gross area. This means that the quality of construction or the amount of space or both must be reduced.

Cost Estimate Analysis

A.	Building Costs	200,000 S.F. at $55.00 S.F.	$11,000,000
B.	Fixed Equipment	(8% of A)	880,000
C.	Site Development	(15% of A)	1,650,000
D.	**Total Construction**	(A + B + C)	**$13,530,000**
E.	Site Acquisition/Demolition		500,000
F.	Moveable Equipment	(8% of A)	880,000
G.	Professional Fees	(6% of D)	811,800
H.	Contingencies	(10% of D)	1,353,000
J.	Administrative Costs	(1% of D)	135,300
K.	**Total Budget Required**	(D + E thru J)	**$17,210,100**

State The PROBLEM

Programming is a process leading to an explicit statement of an architectural problem. It's the hand-off package — from programmer to designer.

After pondering information derived from previous steps, *designer and programmer must write down* the most salient statements regarding the problem, the kind of statements that will shape the building. These, if skillfully composed, can serve as **premises for design,** and later as **design criteria** to evaluate the design solution.

There should be a minimum of four statements concerning the four major considerations, components of the whole problem: Function, Form, Economy and Time. Typically they cover the functional program, the site, the budget and the implications of time. Rarely should there be more than ten statements. More than this would indicate that the problem is still too complex or that minor details are being used as premises for design. Statements must represent the essence of the problem.

The problem statements must be clear and concise—in the *designer's own words* so there is no doubt that he understands. The problem statements should focus on the obvious—which is often overlooked. Stress the uniqueness of the project.

The format for a problem statement can vary with individual designers, but it is good practice to acknowledge a significant and specific condition and establish a general direction for design. While each condition must be precisely stated, the direction (what should be done) should be ambiguous enough to avoid the feeling of being locked into one solution. This direction should be made in terms of performance, so as not to close the door to alternative solutions nor to different expressions in architectural form.

These qualitative statements relate to the whole problem by including all the complicating factors; yet they must represent the essence of the previous steps. They anticipate a comprehensive solution to the whole problem—not by discarding the information in the previous steps (which is kept on display) but by resolving the initial complexity of the design problem into simple and clear statements. The act of resolution pervades the programming process, but it is most vividly expressed in this fifth step. Resolution requires an intensity of intellectual effort. It is hard work to simplify and clarify the statement of the problem; yet this is necessary so that everyone on the project team can cooperate toward the same end.

Programming Principles

To reinforce the concept of Architecture by Team, Bill Caudill developed two principles:

A. **The Principle of Product**
A product has a much better chance of being successful if, during the design, the four major considerations (function, form, economy, and time) are regarded simultaneously.

B. **The Principle of Process**
Every task requires three kinds of thinking action relating to the disciplines of architectural practice: management, design and technology. Teamwork is in the overlap.

The principles described below are closely related to these two principles. They apply specifically to programming.

1. **The Principle of Client Involvement**
The client is a participating member of the project team and makes most decisions at programming.

2. **The Principle of Effective Communication**
Clients and designers require graphic analysis to understand the magnitude of numbers and the implications of ideas.

3. **The Principle of Comprehensive Analysis**
The whole problem covers a wide range of factors which influence design, but they can all be classified in a simple framework of 5 steps and 4 considerations.

4. **The Principle of Bare Essentials**
Programming requires abstracting—distilling—to the essence to bring out only the major aspects of information.

5. **The Principle of Abstract Thinking**
Programming deals with abstract ideas known as programmatic concepts, which are intended mainly as operational solutions to clients' performance problems, without regard to the physical design response.

6. **The Principle of Distinct Separation**
The problem seeking method requires a distinct separation of programming and design—of analysis and synthesis—recognizing them as two different processes calling for different ways of thinking.

7. **The Principle of Efficient Operation**
The programming team requires good management, clear roles and responsibilities, a common language, and standard procedures.

8. **The Principle of Qualitative Information**
The requirements of a proposed building include the clients' goals (what is to be achieved) and concepts (how it is to be achieved).

9. **The Principle of Quantitative Information**
Certain project facts and needs are essentially numerical—numbers of people and things generate area numbers and cost numbers—and they can lead to cost control and a balanced budget with or without the use of computers.

10. **The Principle of Definite Closure**
Programming is a process leading to an explicit statement of an architectural problem—compensating for the missing parts and resolving the initial complexity to simple and clear statements.

In A Nutshell

Programming **IS** a five-step procedure (Goals, Facts, Concepts, Needs, Problem) involving four considerations (Function, Form, Economy, Time).

Programming **IS** a process leading to the statement of an architectural problem and the requirements to be met in offering a solution.

Programming **IS** the process of probing for sufficient information to understand and define the problem.

Programming **IS** problem seeking; design is problem solving.

Programming **IS** providing a sound basis for responsive design.

Programming **IS** analysis; design is synthesis.

Programming **IS NOT** design.

Programming **IS** distinct and separate from design.

Programming **IS** the prelude to good design.

Programming **IS NOT** merely asking questions.

Programming **IS** based on a combination of interviews for data gathering and work sessions for decision making.

Programming **IS NOT** an algorithmic process; it is a heuristic process.

Programming **IS** finding out what the whole problem is.

Programming **IS** the basis for a more comprehensive solution.

Programming **IS** a two-phase process.

Programming **IS** the establishment of limits and the scope of possibilities.

Programming **IS** processing raw data into useful and essential information.

Programming **IS** getting to the essence.

Programming **IS** the same process for any building type.

Programming **IS** essential regardless of size of project or the size of the firm.

Programming **IS** a cooperative process emphasizing client decision making.

Programming **IS** a rational and explicit process in which decisions and information are displayed for close scrutiny.

Programming **IS** an opportunity to raise the client's appreciation and aspiration for better buildings.

Programming **IS** a process requiring a high degree of communication.

Programming **IS NOT** just making a list of wanted spaces.

Programming **IS** the process of distinguishing between wants and needs.

Programming **IS** determining present and future needs.

Part Two

The Appendix

Introduction

The Appendix contains a collection of supplemental material which would have complicated the content of the Primer.

Glossaries and Examples

First, there is a series of seven glossaries dedicated to the general theory and process, to considerations, and to each of the five steps: Goals, Facts, Concepts, Needs and Problems.

Each glossary is used to define terms in the text, but also to define related terms not in the text. The terms are not in alphabetical order because it is more important to explain their interrelationships. For example: Values, Beliefs and Issues are grouped to explain their relationship to Goals. To find a definition, then, first look in the Index; it will cite the proper glossary page.

Programming Procedures

The Information Index uses key and evocative words and phrases to trigger specific questions in the context of the project at hand. Behind these key words are detailed procedures which are universal enough to be negotiable for different building types. These key words are charged with meaning; and that meaning is found in the procedures.

Sophistication, Situations and Simplifications

The Primer covers the basic programming process. The Appendix introduces three short sections explaining (1) the four levels of sophistication which describe the increasing complexity of projects, (2) the variable conditions under which programming services must be provided, and (3) the three ways to simplify design problems. In effect, with all the complexities and the different situations, there must be an optimistic attitude toward making design problems manageable.

Useful Techniques

The most important techniques in programming deal with methods of communication with the client and later with the designer. These include how to interview the client for information and how to use that information during decision-making work sessions. Graphic techniques are required to help clients and designers understand the magnitude of numbers and the implication of ideas. Two such techniques are presented: analysis cards and brown sheets.

Programming reports are often required for program approval. What better order for the sections in the report than those reasonable steps the client followed in the programming process?

The criteria to determine when to use new automated techniques should also help to understand the proper use of the computer during the programming phase.

Ultimately one should be able to evaluate the programming package—without reference to the resulting design. Is it a good architectural program? Use a question set and find out.

Glossaries and Examples

The following Glossaries contain more than definitions of terms with very special usage in architectural programming. They contain examples to illustrate the terms themselves, and also examples of related terms to show their relationships. They contain information linking the technical terms to the process—linking meaning and usage. The Glossary on Needs is perhaps the most complex case of definitions and process. The components of a cost estimate analysis lead to typical control items, to the variations of building efficiency and finally to the mysteries of quality levels.

Glossary on Theory and Process

Architectural Programming: A process leading to the statement of an architectural problem and the requirements to be met in offering a solution.

Systems Analysis: The process of studying an activity typically by mathematical means in order to determine its essential end and how this may most efficiently be attained.

Scientific Method: The principles and procedures used in the systematic pursuit of intersubjectively accessible knowledge and involv-

ing, as necessary conditions:

(1) the recognition and formulation of a problem
(2) the collection of data through observation and, possibly, experiment
(3) the formulation of hypothesis and
(4) the testing for confirmation of the hypothesis formulated.

Traditional Problem Solving Steps:*

(1) Definition of the problem
(2) Establishment of objectives
(3) Collection of data
(4) Analysis of the problem
(5) Consideration of solutions
(6) Solution of the problem

Hypothesis: A proposition, condition or principle which is assumed, without belief, in order to draw out its logical consequences and by this method to test its accord with facts which are known or may be determined.

Analysis: Separation or breaking up of a whole into its fundamental elements or component parts.

Synthesis: Composition or combination of parts or elements so as to form a coherent whole.

Research: Critical and exhaustive investigation or experimentation having for its aim the

*Compare with the five problem seeking steps.

discovery of new facts and their correct interpretation.

Operations Research: The application of scientific and especially mathematical methods to the study and analysis of complex overall problems.

Theory: Principles and generalizations plus their interrelationships that present a clear, rounded and systematic view of a complex problem or field.

Principle: An empirically derived conclusion about irreducible qualities of a system. The particular abstractions that summarize the phenomena of a given subject field.

Generalization: A general statement, law, principle, or proposition.

Generalize: To derive or induce (a general conception or principle) from particulars.

Induction: Reasoning from a part to a whole, from particulars to generals, from individual to the universal.

Deduction: Deriving a conclusion by reasoning. Inferring from a general principle.

Reductionism: A procedure or theory that reduces complex data or phenomena to simple terms.

Resolution: The process of reducing to simpler form. The art of analyzing or converting a complex notion into a simpler one or into its elements.

Heuristic: Serving to guide, discover or reveal. Valuable for stimulating or conducting empirical research but unproved or incapable of proof.

Algorithm: A rule or procedure for solving a mathematical problem that frequently involves repetition of an operation.

Comprehensive: Covering a matter under consideration completely or nearly completely, accounting for all, or virtually all, pertinent considerations.

Complex: Combining various parts. Considerable study, knowledge, experience are needed for comprehension or operation.

Complicated: May heighten notions of difficulty in understanding.

Organize: To put in readiness for cooperative action.

To arrange elements into a whole of inter-dependent parts.

Unorganized: Not brought into a coherent or well-ordered whole.

Simplism: Oversimplification: The tendency to concentrate on a single aspect (as of a problem) to the exclusion of all complicating factors.

Method: A particular approach to problems of truth or knowledge; a systematic procedure, technique or mode of inquiry employed by a particular discipline.

Methodology: The approaches employed in the solution of a problem; a branch of logic that analyzes the procedures that should guide inquiry in a particular field. Methods of inquiry, techniques, procedures used in a particular field.

Reasonable: Carries a much weaker implication of the power to reason in general. Rather refers to actions or decisions or choices that are practical, sensible, just or fair.

Rational: Power to make logical inferences and draw conclusions that enable one to understand the world about him and relate such knowledge to the attainment of goals.

Logical: That which is in harmony with sound reasoning and agrees with accepted principles of logic.

Logic: The science of correct reasoning that deals with the criteria of validity in thought and demonstration.

Key Words: Words with a crucial meaning.

Evocative Words: Words which trigger useful information; charged with emotion as well as meaning and tending to evoke ideas or associations.

Coded Words: Words assigned to arbitrary meanings.

Framework: An open work frame. A frame of reference. A systematic set of relationships.

Information Index: A matrix or rectangular format of key and evocative words arranged to express the relationships of steps and considerations and the typical classification of pertinent information.

Total Project Delivery System: A complete series of operations leading to the occupancy of a completed building: (1) programming (P), (2) schematic design (SD), (3) design development (DD), (4) construction documents (CD), (5) bidding, and (6) construction.

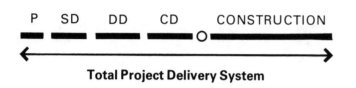

Total Project Delivery System

Total Design Process: The first three phases in architectural practice: (1) programming, (2) schematic design and (3) design development. Programming is a part of the total design process in this definition, but it is separate from schematic design.

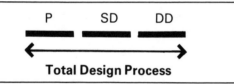

Total Design Process

Design: The second and third phases of the total design process: schematic design and design development.

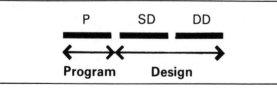

Schematic Design: Interpretation of the owner's project requirements by studies and drawings which illustrate basic architectural concepts, space requirements and relationships, primary circulation, scale, massing, use of site, general appearance and scope of the project. Included is a statement of adequacy of the stipulated project budget.

Design Development: Following approval of schematic design, development includes determination, design and coordination of architectural, structural, mechanical, electrical systems; equipment layouts, and all related site development. This phase results in drawings and documentation, plus additional material as necessary to illustrate "final" development and insure that all significant design questions and/or problems have been answered.

Construction Documents: This phase transforms the preceding approved "DD Package" into a set of detailed, legal, bidding documents which relate to the construction industry. These documents control and direct the construction process via construction drawings and detail materials/building systems specifications.

Glossary on Considerations

Considerations: Relate to an architectural product and indicate the four major types of information needed in programming.

Content: Refers to four considerations which

comprise a comprehensive architectural problem: Function, Form, Economy and Time.

Function: How the design product will work to do the job it is supposed to do. The performance.

The "Do"—the way people and things will move about to do the tasks they have to do.

Functions: The action for which a person or thing is specially fitted, used or responsible, or for which it exists.

Functional: Designed chiefly from the point of view of use: utilitarian work, operations, performance.

Activities: An organized unit for performing a specific function.

Form: In design, form means the shape and structure of a building as distinguished from its materials. It is what you see and feel.

In programming, form refers to what you will see and feel, avoiding the suggestion of a design solution. It's the "what is there now" and "what will be there".

Economy: The efficient and sparing use of the means available for the end proposed. Implies an interest in achieving maximum results from the initial budget and the maximum cost/effectiveness of the operating and life cycle costs.

Time: Deals with the influence of history, the inevitability of change from the present, and with projections into the future.

Operational: Refers to goals and concepts dealing with the process—how the client/architect team will proceed through the total project delivery system to fulfill the contract.

Glossary on Goals

Goal: The end toward which effort is directed. Suggests something attained only by prolonged effort.

Goals can be classified as (1) project goals, and (2) operational goals.

Project goals are concerned with product; operational goals are concerned with process.

Project Goals are established by the client working with the architect. These are elicited from the considerations of Function, Form, Economy and Time...and their sub-categories.

The following can be used as synonyms for the term "goals": objectives, aims, missions, purposes, reasons, philosophies, aspirations, policies.

Any of these terms can be used to generate statements which specify what is to be achieved toward the success of the project—what the client wants to accomplish and why.

Consider the following use of these commonly used synonyms for the word "Goal":

Objective: A more detailed delineation of a particular goal. Implies something tangible and immediately attainable.

Goals tend to be general; objectives tend to be specific.

Objectives are more time bound and quantitative—and therefore a better measure for evaluating the degree of achievement than generalized goals.

Example:

Goal: *To serve as many students from the state of Texas as possible.*

Objective: *To increase enrollment by the amount of 1,000 students per year.*

Policy: A definite course of action selected from among alternatives and in the light of given conditions to guide and determine present and future decisions.

Policies are rules or guidelines which implement goals and objectives. While a goal or an objective stresses the effort of action, a policy represents a selected course of action.

Example:

Goal: *To promote academic efficiency.*

Objective: *To reduce student travel time between classes.*

Policy: *That service courses be decentralized where desirable.*

Concept: *Decentralized clusters of activity.*

Concepts are functional or organizational ideas which also implement goals and objectives. While policies are classified under goals, concepts are not.

Intention: A determination to act in a certain way. Implies little more than what one has in mind to do or bring about.

Aim: Something intended or desired to be attained by one's effort. Implies effort directed toward attaining or accomplishing.

PROJECT GOALS

1. **Function**
   a. **Mission Statement**
      (1) **Explains Reasons**
      (2) **Answers Why**
      (3) **States Purpose**
   b. **Philosophy**
2. **Form**
3. **Economy**
4. **Time**

Mission: A task or function assigned or undertaken.

A mission statement of an organization simply explains the reason for its existence.

A functional goal answers the question why?

It should state the purpose of the organization to provide guidance to all subordinate programs and activities.

Example:

This university's mission is to build knowledge and to prepare the future leadership for change and improvement.

The mission statements should include the general functions or services to be performed, without anticipating implementing concepts.

Example:

The functions of a university are: (1) *teaching,* (2) *research and* (3) *service.*

End: The goal toward which an agent should act. Stresses the intended effect of action often in distinction to the action or means as such.

Philosophy: A basic theory concerning a particular subject, process, or sphere of activity. Asking the client for the philosophy behind the functional program often results in answers and information that are too esoteric and too vague to be directly useful.

Purpose: Something set up as an end to be attained. Suggests a more settled determination.

Aspirations: (1) A goal aspired to, (2) A condition strongly desired. The latter indicates the informality with which a goal can be stated.

Top management responsible for comprehensive planning will necessarily establish the broadest project goals, while middle management will develop more specific goals...consistent with the broad goals. The user usually establishes objectives.

Project goals can be established with no immediate means of achievement available. However, it might be well to remember that goals must eventually be tested to determine their integrity and usefulness—depending on means of achievement.

PROJECT GOALS

1. "Motherhood"
2. Lip-Service
3. Inspirational
4. Practical

Consider the following kinds of project goals:

"Motherhood" Goals: These are unassailable goals; however, they are too general to be directly useful.

Example:

To provide a good environment for children.

Lip-Service Goals: These are show-pieces that look good in a public relations publication but after testing are found lacking in sufficient backup for accomplishment.

Inspirational Goals: These are general "Motherhood" goals whose ambiguity may serve to trigger the designer's subconscious to uncover a design concept.

Example:

To project the dynamic, progressive spirit of the bank.

Practical Goals: These goals may provide guidance to the collection of pertinent facts.

They are intended to be accomplished through known concepts and may well affect the statement of the problem.

Example:

Goal: *To help maintain the individual student's sense of identity within the large mass of enrollments.*

Fact: *Enrollments in this school will grow from the initial 1,000 students to 2,700 students.*

Concept: *Decentralize the mass of 2,700 students into schools of 900 students with four houses within each school.*

Goals are derived from values, beliefs, issues, either consciously or unconsciously. In fact, with a client/user who is not goal-oriented or is even non-verbal, it might be easier to bring out values, beliefs, and/or issues which may lead to goals.

Value: Something intrinsically valuable or desirable. Relative worth, utility, or importance. Aims and objectives that act as a basis for motivation. Basic interests or motives.

Value: *The worth of the individual as a human being.*

Goal: *To help maintain the individual student's sense of identity within the large mass of enrollments.*

Issue: A point of debate or controversy. A matter that is in dispute between parties.

Issue: *The racial issue.*

Goal: *To develop the performing arts to such an outstanding level that all races will be attracted to this school.*

Belief: Mental acceptance of something offered as true, with or without certainty.

Belief: *That a better environment can help people live better lives.*

Goal: *To produce forms and spaces with the quality of architecture.*

OPERATIONAL GOALS

1. **Time**
2. **People**
3. **Cost**
4. **Information**
5. **Techniques**
6. **Location**

Operational Goals generally result from the architect's contract or from operational decisions made by the client/architect team. These goals will affect how the team will proceed through the project to fulfill the contract. They will give rise to operational concepts.

Operational goals describe what the team wants to accomplish in terms of the total project delivery system—the process, not the product.

The effort is to identify the best possible course of action in terms of time, people, and cost, and often in terms of information, techniques and location.

Examples of operational goals:

Time: *To occupy the finished building by September 1978.*

Time and Location: *To keep the present hospital operational while the new wing is being constructed.*

Information and Techniques: *To process enrollment/space data.*

Time and Technique: *To develop a schedule which will compress the total project delivery time.*

Cost: *To effect a 20% gross profit on the whole project.*

People: *To coordinate the team's activities to make the most effective use of consultants.*

Glossary on Facts

Information: Knowledge obtained from investigation, study or instruction.

Fact: Information presented as having objective reality; truth.

Data: Factual material used as a basis for reasoning, discussion or decision.

Relevant: Properly applying to the matter at hand. Having a (logical) connection with a matter under consideration.

Pertinent: Interchangeable with relevant. Often stresses a more significant relationship which contributes to the understanding of a problem or matter at hand.

Assumption: A statement accepted or supposed true without proof or demonstration. In programming classified under facts as assumed hard facts or fixed opinions.

Truth: Conformity to knowledge, fact, actuality, or logic.

Empirical: Based on factual information; observation or direct sense experience as opposed to theoretical knowledge.

User Characteristics: Those physical, social, emotional and intellectual qualities which typify the users and affect their behavior patterns.

Those common characteristics including physical size, age and sex, social class, likes and dislikes, intellectual ability.

Parameter: Mathematical term for a symbolic quantity that may be associated with some measurable quantity in the real world...such as cost/sq. ft.

An arbitrary constant characterizing by each of its particular values some particular member of a system.

Disinterestedness: An objectivity toward uncovering of information; detached scrutiny.

Objectivity: The use of facts without distortion by personal feelings or prejudices.

Skepticism: Suspension of judgement until all the data is analyzed.

Glossary on Concepts

Concept: Something conceived in the mind: idea, notion.

Programmatic Concepts refer to ideas intended mainly as functional and organizational solutions to the client's own performance problems. They are general or abstract ideas generalized from particular instances.

Design Concepts refer to ideas intended as physical solutions to the client's architectural problems.

Example:

Programmatic Concept: *Decentralize the mass of 2,700 students into schools of 900 students with four houses within each school.*

Design Concepts: *The physical responses to the programmatic concept of decentralization above may be: (1) the dispersion of three buildings, (2) the dispersion/compactness of three floors in one building, or (3) the compactness of a single building with three identifiable schools on one floor.*

PROJECT GOALS (Ends)

PROGRAMMATIC CONCEPTS (Means)

DESIGN CONCEPTS (Response)

In programming, programmatic concepts are emphasized and design concepts avoided. It is essential to understand the difference between these two kinds of concepts.

To deal with design concepts during programming would mean: (1) jumping to conclusions, (2) synthesizing too early, (3) and determining sub-solutions before the sub-problems were identified.

Programmatic concepts attempt to implement practical goals. They are a means of accomplishing goals. If goals are ends,

programmatic concepts are means; and design concepts are the physical response to them and to the design premises in the statement of the problem.

Programmatic concepts are further classified under Function, Form, Economy and Time.

Since they are intended as functional and organizational solutions it might be thought that most of them are functional. This is not so.

It might also be thought impossible to avoid the physical aspects of concepts. It may be so, but the intent is to state a programmatic concept in such a way as to elicit alternative responses in design.

Recurring Concepts refer to programmatic concepts which not only appear in just one project or type of institution, but also appear as potential aspects of any project or institution. These concepts then are worth testing in any project to find their applicability.

Operational Concepts refer to ideas intended as procedural solutions to the client/architect team's procedural problems. This concept indicates how the team will proceed through the project to fulfill the client/architect contract.

Operational concepts implement operational goals in terms of time, people, and cost, and often in terms of information, techniques and location.

Examples of Operational Goals and Concepts:

Operational Goal: *To occupy the finished building by September 1978.*

Operational Concept: *Scheduling and critical path method.*

Operational Goal: *To keep the present hospital operational while the new wing is being constructed.*

Operational Concept: *Concurrent activities.*

Operational Goal: *To process enrollment/space data.*

Operational Concept: *Automation*

Operational Goal: *To develop a schedule which will compress the total project delivery time.*

Operational Concept: *Concurrent scheduling.*

Operational Goal: *To effect a 20% percent gross profit on the whole architectural project.*

Operational Concept: *Management*

Operational Goal: *To coordinate the team's activities to make the most effective use of consultants.*

Operational Concept: *Team action.*

Glossary on Needs

Needs: Requirements; something necessary; an indispensable or essential thing or quality.

Wants: Something lacking and desired or wished for.

Requirement: Something wanted or needed.

Space Requirement: Detailed listing of the amounts of each type of space designated for a specific purpose.

Performance: Something accomplished or carried out. The execution of an action that fulfills agreed-upon requirements.

Performance Requirements: Those requirements stemming from the unique user needs in terms of the physical, social and psychological environment to be provided. These will involve the adequacy, the quality and the organization of space.

Functional Requirements: Those requirements dealing chiefly with the way people will use the project with convenience, efficiency and effectiveness. These, also, will involve the adequacy, the quality and the organization of space.

Human Requirements: Those requirements stemming from the generalized human needs in terms of the physical, social and psychological environment to be provided. These human needs involve such general categories as self-preservation, physical comfort, self-image and social affiliation—initially expressed as specific goals.

Cost Estimate Analysis

A. **Building Cost**: Includes all costs of construction within five feet of the building line; all items required by codes (fire extinguishers cabinets, fire alarm systems, etc.); and items normally found in buildings regardless of type (drinking fountains).

B. **Fixed Equipment**: Includes all equipment items which may be installed before completion of the building and which are a part of the construction contract, such as lockers, food service equipment, fixed seating, fixed medical equipment, security equipment, stage equipment, stage lighting, etc.

C. **Site Development**: Includes all work required which lies within the site boundary and five feet from the edge of the building, i.e. grading and fill, fencing, electronic perimeter system, roads and parking, utilities, landscape development, athletic fields, walks, site lighting, street furniture, site graphics, on-site sewage treatment plant, unusual foundation conditions.

D. **Total Construction**: This represents the total budget for construction, usually the contract documents base bid.

E. **Site Acquisition and/or Demolition**: Money budgeted for purchasing the project site and/or demolition of existing structures.

F. **Movable Equipment**: This category includes all movable equipment and furniture items, but does not include operational equipment (i.e. microscopes, library books, etc. purchased from operating funds).

G. **Fees**: Costs of architectural and engineering services and of consultant services.

H. **Contingency**: A percentage of the total construction cost is included to serve as a planning contingency, bidding contingency, and construction reserve (change orders, etc.)

J. **Administrative Costs**: Items the owner is responsible for during the planning process, i.e., legal fees, site survey, soil testing, insurance, material testing.

K. **Total Budget**: This represents the total budget required to occupy the new facility and/or renovated areas.

NOTE: For those projects which require permanent and interim financing costs, the following control items can be listed as separate items under "J":

J (A). **Permanent Financing Costs**: Includes cost of obtaining a loan such as an investment banker fee leading to a bond issue or as a construction loan fee related to a mortgage banker.

J (B). **Interim Financing Cost**: Includes all construction financing costs for borrowing construction funds. The amount varies with construction time.

Typical Control Items

The cost estimate analysis must be as comprehensive and realistic as possible, with no doubt as to what comprises the total budget required. Once the total net area of a project is determined, it is an easy task to arrive at a reasonable efficiency ratio and the total gross area. This area, multiplied by a realistic unit cost, will produce the estimated building cost (Line A) upon which depend estimates of many cost items.

The use of typical percentages as control items will lead to the Total Budget Required (Line K). However, these percentages are not constant; they must be adjusted inversely at the upper and lower levels of unit cost. Nevertheless, the percentages listed below indicate the usual ranges of variation depending on the building type and other factors.

Cost Estimate Analysis

A. Building Costs	197,485 S.F. at $55.00/S.F.	$10,861,694
B. Fixed Equipment	(8% of A)	868,936
C. Site Development	(15% of A)	1,629,254
D. Total Construction	(A+B+C)	$13,359,884
E. Site Acquisition/Demolition		500,000
F. Moveable Equipment	(8% of A)	868,936
G. Professional Fees	(6% of D)	801,593
H. Contingencies	(10% of D)	1,335,988
J. Admin. Costs	(1% of D)	133,599
K. Total Budget Reqd	(D+E thru J)	$17,000,000

A. Building Cost:

Net Area $\div$ Efficiency Ratio = Gross Area

Gross Area x Unit Cost = Building Cost

Example:

60,000 Net SF $\div$ .60 = 100,000 Gross SF

100,000 Gross SF x $30/SF = $3,000,000.00

B. Fixed Equipment:

Percentage of Line A

Low	.5%
Medium	10-15%
High	20%
Specially High	30%

Commercial Office Bldg.	.5- 7%
Sports Center	5%
Elementary School	6-10%
Secondary School	8-12%
University Academic Bldg.	7%
Civic Center	8%
Housing Project	7-10%
University Average Building.	14%
Jail	12-15%
School of Medicine	15%
Hospital	18-20%
University Science Bldg	20%
Civic Auditorium	20-25%
Heavy Industrial Arts	30%
Teaching Dental Lab	30%

C. Site Development:

Percentage of Line A

Low 5%
Medium 10-15%
High 20%
Specially High 30%

Urban Site	5%
Elementary School	6-12%
Secondary school	10-15%
Suburban Site	14-15%
Hospital	10-15%
Secondary School	20%
Extensive Development plus special conditions such as rock excavation, steep slopes, etc.	30%

D. Total Construction Cost:

Sum of A + B + C

E. Site Acquisition and/or Demolition:
Varies widely

F. Movable Equipment:

Percentage of Line A

Low 5%
Medium 10-15%
High 20%

Elementary School	6-10%
Secondary School	8-12%
College	10-15%
Library	15%
Medical Office Bldg.	15%
Hospital	18-20%
Vocational School	20%

G. Professional Fees, Including Consultants:

Percentage of Line D

Vary from 5% to 10%

H. Contingencies:

Low 5%
Medium 10%
High 15%

J. Administrative Costs:

Percentage of Line D

Varies 1% to 2%

K. Total Budget Required:

Sum of D + E + F + G + H + J = K

NOTE: For those projects which require permanent and interim financing costs, the following control items can be listed as separate items under "J":

J(A). **Permanent Financing Cost:**

Percentage of Line K

Investment Banker Fee
   (a) Varies 2.5% to 6%
   (b) Construction Loan Fee
        varies 1% to 2%

J(B). **Interim Financing Cost:**

Percentage of Line D

Varies 1.5% to 2.5% above prime rate per year of construction time...approximately.

Building Cost Indexes

The building cost (line A of the Cost Estimate Analysis) depends on (1) the total net area (the sum of all space needs), (2) a reasonable efficiency ratio of net to gross area, and (3) the cost per square foot escalated to mid-construction.

Types of Quality

Of these, it is the cost per square foot, the unit cost, that is usually associated with the quality of the building. It is true that the cost per square foot represents the quality of materials, systems and construction—the quality of the architectural fabric. But it should come as no surprise that both the total net area and the building efficiency also represent aspects of quality—functional and spatial qualities respectively.

Levels of Quality

But before covering the types of quality in more detail, it is helpful to discuss different levels of quality. It should be obvious that the architect and his client must reach an agreement on the level of quality for the project. The client must be conscious of a wide range of choices.

Automobile Analogy

One useful device is the analogy of automobiles. A client can be expected to understand the difference in quality between a VW Beetle and a Rolls Royce—between an austere and a superb quality—without having to resort to a detailed analysis. To round out the analogy without using trade names, consider the following six levels of quality:

For Automobiles	For Buildings
Super Luxury	Superb
Luxury	Grand
Full	Excellent
Intermediate	Moderate
Compact	Economical
Subcompact	Austere

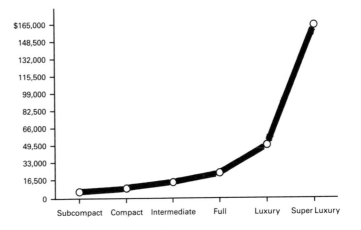

Quality Levels/Unit Costs For Automobiles

The accompanying chart shows the relationship between the unit cost for automobiles and quality level. The unit costs are taken from a consumer publication indicating the "best buys" in each category. Note that the difference in levels is gradual until the last two. The super-luxury level is actually shown at one third of its potential.

The point of the analogy is this: Autos and buildings share the same wide range in levels of quality. They also share similar quality factors, based on (1) materials, systems and construction (2) function and performance, and (3) spatial qualities. Clients and architects must be aware of the wide range in levels of quality and they must agree on a realistic quality level for which funds are available.

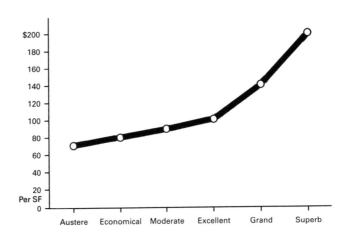

Quality Levels/Unit Costs For Civic Auditoriums

*Based on 1987 costs.

Building Efficiency

Now back to finding a reasonable efficiency ratio of net to gross area, but first some definitions:

Net Assignable Areas: Include the sum of all functional spaces required to serve the basic program.

Unassigned Areas: Consist of all other spaces in the building, specifically circulation areas, mechanical areas, general toilets, janitor closets, unassigned storage, walls and partitions.

Gross Area: Represents essentially the sum of assignable and unassignable areas.

Efficiency Ratio: The ratio of the net assignable area to the unassignable area expressed as percentages of the gross area. In the programming phase, this ratio is used to project the total gross area requirements using the net area requirements as a base.

The simplest method to do this involves dividing the net area by the appropriate percentage representing the net area.

Example: @   60/40% ratio

$$\frac{60,000 \text{ net SF}}{.60} = 100,000 \text{ gross SF}$$

Efficiency and Quality

There is a certain aspect of architectural quality which is inversely proportional to the "plan efficiency" of a building. Therefore, it is important to predict and assign a reasonable efficiency for a building which would contribute to its expected quality.

Common Range

Superb	50/50%
Grand	55/45%
Excellent	60/40%
Moderate	65/35%
Economical	67/33%
Austere	70/30%

Uncommon Range

Meager	75/25%
Spare	80/20%
Minimal	85/15%
Skeletal	90/10%

For example: one of the factors affecting the architectural quality of a civic auditorium is plan efficiency. A civic auditorium intended as a statement of community pride would surely have an efficiency ratio of 50% net floor area to 50% unassigned area, expressed 50/50%. On the other hand, a civic auditorium intended merely as a necessary solution would have an austere 70/30% ratio.

With a superb and an austere building on opposite ends of a scale, a value judgment can be made regarding the quality intended and the reasonable efficiency which can be assumed for planning purposes. Further still, this scale can be expanded to provide a full range of quality levels, but not for the same building type.

Using six levels seems appropriate for most building types; however, they may not be the same six levels or there may be more than six levels. Building services, for example, would start with a skeletal 90/10% depending on the components and on the predominance of warehousing.

Typical Components of Unassigned Space

Allowing for differences in building types among institutional and civic buildings, the distribution of unassigned areas shown below are expressed as typical percentages of the gross area. Office buildings are included in this analysis (usually 50%) when using the same definition of building efficiency as for other building types.

Circulation (Interior not incl. lobby; Exterior Covered; Phantom Corridors)	16.0%	18.0%	20.0%	22.0%	26.0%	30.0%
Mechanical	5.0	5.5	5.5	7.5	8.0	8.0
Walls, Partitions, Structure	7.0	7.0	7.0	8.0	8.5	9.0
Toilets (Public)	1.5	1.5	1.5	1.5	1.5	2.0
Janitor Closets	0.2	0.5	0.5	0.5	0.5	0.5
Unassigned Storage	0.3	0.5	0.5	0.5	0.5	0.5
	30.0%	33.0%	35.0%	40.0%	45.0%	50.0%

Circulation areas include interior corridors, exterior covered walks (½ of full area) and phantom corridors, which are undefined circulation areas through assigned areas, such as a pathway through a programmed lobby space. Note that circulation areas are, by far, the largest single component of unassigned space.

Mechanical areas and walls, partitions and structure can each increase to 12% in monumental buildings.

The other components of unassigned space can vary from 2% to 5% and still not amount to much area.

These percentages can be used as guidelines until reasonable percentages can be assumed for a particular project.

Refer to the "Classification of Building Areas", Publication Number 1235, National Academy of Sciences, National Research Council, Washington, D. C. 1964.

Reasonable Ratios

Differences in predominating room sizes, occupancy levels, circulation requirements and special mechanical requirements lead to different efficiency ratios for various buildings.

For example, the predominance of small rooms requiring higher percentages in circulation and partitions leads to a reasonable efficiency ratio of 55/45% in an administration building.

On the other hand, the large gym areas in physical education would indicate small percentages in circulation and partitions, leading to a reasonable efficiency ratio of 70/30%. When this is influenced by unusually large spectator areas demanding large areas of circulation, ratios of 65/35% and 60/40% can be expected.

Building Types

The following building efficiency ratios are reasonable for the building types listed, until they can be modified by the specific conditions of a particular project.

Home Office Buildings	50/50%
University Administration	55/45%
Corporate R + D	50/50%
University R + D	60/40%
Science	60/40%
Dormitory	60/40%
Student Center	60/40%
Auditorium	60/40%
Museum	65/35%
Library	65/35%
Academic	65/35%
Physical Education	70/30%
Building Services	75/25%

Quality of Construction

The construction quality level is represented by a unit cost figure such as cost per gross square foot. The unit costs typically include architectural, structural, electrical, plumbing and mechanical work, but do not include site development and fixed equipment.

Various national organizations publish timely unit costs based on national averages. They also publish regional modifiers or location factors for each state ... and even for individual cities. To adjust the unit cost for a particular building type (based on national averages) for the specific location, the unit cost is multiplied by the location factor for the city. Further, this adjusted unit cost must be escalated by a reasonable percentage per year projected to mid-way through the construction period.

The average unit costs are typically identified with different types of construction related to fire ratings, but these average unit costs represent only the average quality level of construction in each type. The average quality represents good standard construction with adequate mechanical and electrical services and an average level of finishes. These average unit costs can be used to advantage; however, there is a great need to know a wider range of unit costs than those representing national averages. The chart below indicates the possibility of six choices in quality — ranging from austere to superb. Unit costs become obsolete in time.

Building Type	Austere	Economical	Moderate	Excellent	Grand	Superb
Civic Auditoriums	$70	$80	$ 90	$100	$140	$200
Research Laboratories	75	90	105	120	145	180
Correctional Facilities	50	70	90	110	135	160
Hospitals	50	70	90	110	135	160
Offices	35	50	70	90	115	150
Libraries	50	60	70	80	100	150
Civic Centers	50	60	70	80	100	150
Education Facilities	35	45	55	65	80	105
Warehouses	20	25	30	35	45	60

Approximate cost per square foot as of January 1987

The chart can be used only as a heuristic device to find the appropriate level of quality for a project and to be aware of the wide range of unit costs. National averages usually span over three of these unit cost figures—most often in the lower end of the range. The level of quality depends on the level of construction, mechanical and electrical services and interior/exterior finishes.

It is important to remember that these unit costs must be adjusted to the state and preferably to the city of the project. To do this, multiply the unit cost by the location factor. For example, $30.00 per square foot must be multiplied by 1.08 to adjust the unit cost to Kansas ... $32.40 per square foot. Further, if escalation is estimated at 8% per year and midway through construction is estimated at two years, then $32.40 is multiplied by 16% for an escalated unit cost of $37.58 per square foot.

Civic auditoriums range from high school auditoriums used by the community to halls for the performing arts. Their unit costs represent a wide range in levels of quality.

Offices also have a wide range of types: low rise offices, high rise offices, medical offices, municipal offices. Most of the average unit costs are in the three or four lower levels, but if the client wants superb facilities, the highest level is indicated.

Under educational facilities, the wide range of unit costs can be justified by the wide range in educational levels: elementary schools, secondary schools, community colleges and university buildings.

While warehouses have unit costs covering the lower ranges because they are not usually of high quality in construction, services and finishes, there are those warehouses which are the exception.

Functional Adequacy

The six levels of quality are also applicable to the functional adequacy of a building. Theoretically, it refers to the total net area per unit. Actually most references of this type are made in gross area per unit — which is complicated by a variable building efficiency that makes comparisons difficult.

Nevertheless, this area per unit is intended to indicate the level of service and support per unit. Here are some examples: the area per bed in a hospital, the area per student in a high school, college or university, the area per seat in an auditorium.

A 1500 student high school, with a building efficiency of 65/35%, could have an austere 120 sq. ft. per student but without an auditorium and a spectator gym. It could have a moderate 140 sq. ft. per student but with limited vocational facilities. The superb 200 sq. ft. per student would include educational enrichments *wanted* by many communities. The student capacity of the school is an important factor related to the central service facilities. A 1000-student high school would have higher areas per student and a 2000-student school, lower areas.

Similarly, an auditorium would have a wide range in levels — from an austere 20 sq. ft. per seat to a superb 90 sq. ft. per seat — for the same general capacity of 2500 seats. Again, the capacity is an important factor. A 500 seat auditorium would have a higher range in levels — higher areas per seat. Refer to the chart showing the 20 sq. ft. to 90 sq. ft. per seat range. The austere 20 sq. ft. per seat would indicate limited lobbies, offices, storage, stage and backstage facilities. These facilities would all increase with the rising levels of quality, even to include public restaurants.

Summary

Consider the six levels of quality and the automobile analogy only as heuristic devices to expand the usual narrow range of quality levels and to establish the appropriate level of quality for a project. These might help both the client and the designer to strive for the same appropriate level among the *kinds* of quality. This would avoid the total mismatch of a VW Beetle body with a Rolls Royce engine — although some inconsistency may be necessary to balance the budget.

The example of civic auditoriums is shown in the accompanying chart. It can be assumed that a small total budget imposes a low unit cost and area per seat — which, in turn, affect the efficiency ratio. Compare the figures for the austere quality with those of the grand quality; note that while the gross areas have a ratio of 1:3, the net areas resulting from the different efficiency ratios have a ratio of 1:2, and the unit costs also have a ratio of 1:2. This would indicate that a higher increase in quality corresponds to the amount of unassigned areas. This could be said to be an inconsistency, but it is definitely a part of the grand quality.

Civic Auditoriums within a 2000-3000 Seat Capacity Range

Kinds of Quality	Austere	Economical	Moderate	Excellent	Grand	Superb
Gross Area/Seat	20 S.F.	25 S.F.	30 S.F.	40 S.F.	60 S.F.	90 S.F.
Efficiency Ratio	70/30%	67/33%	65/35%	60/40%	55/45%	50/50%
Cost per S.F.	$70	$80	$90	$100	$140	$200

Guidelines for
Site Development Costs

Site development costs vary widely depending on the requirements of the building type, the nature and location of the site and the quality level of the development. Site development costs vary from a low of 5% of the building cost and a medium level between 10% — 15% to a high of 20%. The especially high percentage of 30% allows for extraordinary conditions such as rock excavation, very steep slopes and intensive development requirements.

Before a detailed analysis can be made based on a specific master plan or schematic design, it may be useful to list the possible components of site development costs and their approximate percentages of the building cost. The twelve components listed below may be used as a heuristic device to justify the selection of a specific percentage—which can be refined with successive approximations and more detailed information.

1. **Site Preparation**

   Estimate 1% to 3% of building costs.

2. **Parking**

   Allow 125 cars per acre = 350 sq. ft. /car
   Estimate lump sum per car.

3. **Roadways**

   Estimate lump sum per linear foot

4. **Sidewalks and Terraces**

   Estimate 1% to 7% of building cost.

5. **Walls and Screens**

   Estimate .5% to 2.5% of building cost.

6. **Outdoor Sports Facilities**

   Estimate lump sum per unit and type.

7. **On-Site Utilities**

   Estimate 1% to 3% of building cost

8. **Off-Site Utilities** (if required)

   Estimate 3% to 5% of building cost

9. **Storm Drainage**

   Estimate .5% to 2.5% of building cost.

10. **Landscaping**

    Estimate planting 1% to 2% of building cost.

11. **Outdoor Equipment**

    Estimate lump sum.

12. **Outdoor Lighting**

    Estimate pedestrian lighting 1% of building cost, and parking lighting lump sum per car

How to Work Back From Total Budget to Building Cost

Even before the total gross area can be determined from the space program, it may be judicious to start with the available funds as being the total budget (Line K) and to work back to building cost (Line A) to find the approximate area that may be feasible to build within the total budget. This could be the first trial run of several required to balance the budget.

The following formula can be used to reduce Line K, Total Budget Required, to Line A, Building Cost:

$$\text{Building Cost} = \frac{\text{Total Budget - Site Acquisition}}{X + Y + Z}$$

$X = 1 + ($____% Fixed Eqpt$) + ($____% Site Dev$)$

$Y = (X)[($____% Contingency$) + ($____% Prof Fee$) + ($____% Admin Cost$)]$

$Z = $____% Movable Equipment

NOTE: Percentages expressed as follows:
15% = .15

Where necessary, interim financing percentage is added to Admin Cost. Permanent financing percentage becomes T in $X + Y + Z + T$

Cost Estimate Analysis

A. Building Costs	197,485 S.F. at $55.00/S.F.	$10,861,694
B. Fixed Equipment	(8% of A)	868,936
C. Site Development	(15% of A)	1,629,254
D. Total Construction	(A+B+C)	$13,359,884
E. Site Acquisition/Demolition		500,000
F. Moveable Equipment	(8% of A)	868,936
G. Professional Fees	(6% of D)	801,593
H. Contingencies	(10% of D)	1,335,988
J. Admin. Costs	(1% of D)	133,599
K. Total Budget Reqd	(D+E thru J)	$17,000,000

Trial Run Calculation

Given:

Total Budget = $17,000,000

Site Acquisition = $500,000

$X = 1 + (.08$ Fixed Eqpt) $ + (.15$ Site Dev)
$= 1.23$

$Y = 1.23 \times (.10$ Cont) $ + (.06$ Prof Fee) $ + (.01$ Admin)
$= .2091$

$Z = .08$ Movable Equip
$= .08$

Line A $= \dfrac{\text{Total Budget - Site Acquisition}}{X + Y + Z}$

$= \dfrac{\$17,000,000 - \$500,000}{1.23 + .2091 + .08}$

$= \dfrac{\$16,500,000}{1.5191}$

$= \$10,861,694$

Gross SF = Line A $\div$ Cost/SF

$= \$10,861,694 \div \$55/\text{SF}$

$= 197,485$ SF

These calculations indicate that the total budget will afford a building project of approximately 197,485 sq. ft.—based upon the given percentages as control items.

Glossary on Statement of the Problem

Problem Statement: A description of the critical conditions and design premises which become the starting point for Schematic Design.

Hypothesis: An assumed or real condition taken as a basis for inference or ground from which to draw conclusions.

Condition: Something established or agreed upon as a requisite to the doing of something else.

Premise: A condition stated as leading to a conclusion.

Design Premise: A specific condition leading to a general design directive.

Criteria: The standards by which performances are tested or judged.

Design Criteria: The problem statements in terms of design premises are used as standards to judge a design solution.

Abstract (Adj.): Having no reference to a thing or things: opposed to concrete.

Abstract (Noun): A synopsis or an epitome concentrated essence of a larger whole, after filtering out unneeded details.

Essence: The intrinsic of indispensable properties, the essential nature, of a thing.

Actual Examples of Statements of the Problem

The following pages contain statements of the problem from actual projects covering different building types and written by different programmer/designer teams. Note the different styles and formats—even different titles: problem statements, design premises, design goals. Some are very concise; others are very wordy. Most of them follow the format of identifying a condition leading to a general design directive.

For comparative reasons, all of these statements were rearranged to follow the same order: Function, Form, Economy, Time and Operational—even if this destroyed an intentional priority. Perhaps it is unfair to the teams to exhibit their statements outside the context of the rest of the program; the statements were not intended to stand alone.

Many times the wording is coded to a meaning assigned by the architect/client team very early to procure brevity in repeated references. These coded words may make it obvious that these statements were not intended to be published beyond those initiated into the team. They remain unedited and without the benefit of hindsight. They are working items with a task limited to the specific project at hand; however, references to clients and the location of their projects were deleted.

The date of the project was included to provide some reference to prevailing conditions. For example, in 1951, school design emphasized natural cross ventilation and not air conditioning. The Six Salient Considerations for the design of the senior high school (1950) also reflect the prevailing educational thought that secondary education had not yet begun to change.

The statements are uneven in significance—even within a project. However, they were selected as actual sets representing a variety of differences and they show that there is room for improvement in the clarity of thinking and expression, as well as in the ability to extract the essence without leaving out the critical form givers.

MIDDLE SCHOOL
Schematic Design
Date of Project: Feb 1976

DESIGN PREMISES

FUNCTION

Since the organizational structure is to be departmentalized within an open plan, **the design should provide for some physical identity for each subject group without establishing definite boundaries or limits.**

FORM

Since the school should provide for the total needs of the student, **the design should facilitate the unscheduled social interaction of students as well as the scheduled educational activities.**

ECONOMY

The project budget is fixed and allows for a building cost of $23.00/square foot; therefore, **the quality of building systems, materials and finishes must be balanced within the budget without sacrificing durability, maintenance and operating costs.**

TIME

Since the educational requirements will likely change many times during the life of the school, **the facility must accommodate changes in educational philosophy, teaching methods and techniques.**

MILITARY ACADEMY
Master Plan
Date of Project: Nov 1974
PROBLEM STATEMENT

FUNCTION
Since the emphasis must be placed on pedestrian movement in the cadet zone and in the family housing/community service center, **the master plan must provide for the separation of pedestrian movement and vehicular traffic.**

Since the predominant cadet formation will be a company with platoons in line, **the master plan should respond with broad aprons and sidewalks.**

FORM
Since the cadet zone must locate facilities within a 5-6 minute walking distance, **the master plan must respond with the appropriate density.**

Since the climatic conditions are rigorous during the summer months, **the master plan must respond with short walking distances and shaded areas to encourage pedestrian traffic.**

Since the area is barren and austere, **the master plan should create green planted areas for the psychological effect.**

Since the projected image of the Academic Campus must reflect the military values of strength, order and discipline, **the master plan should respond to this image.**

ECONOMY
Since the Academy will be a military showcase, **the quality of design and construction must be of a high level.**

TIME
Since the Academy may grow even beyond the two planned phases, **the master plan must allow an open-ended framework for expansion.**

SENIOR HIGH SCHOOL
Schematic Design
Date of Project: Dec 1950

SIX SALIENT CONSIDERATIONS FOR DESIGN

FUNCTION

That students spend as much time in halls (over an hour a day) as they do in any one classroom or laboratory. Therefore, halls and other circulation elements should be designed to help achieve the aims of the educational program. **(Note:** Perhaps this consideration provides the fundamental difference between the high school plant and the elementary school plant.)

That the school plant will be used the year around for community improvement, education and recreation. Therefore, the school plant should be designed to facilitate community use. Translated into planning techniques, this means proper zoning of the main architectural elements. For example, those elements which are to be used by both students and the public, such as the gymnasium and auditorium, should be grouped in one zone for efficient use and economical maintenance.

That the school plant should be a real social center for boys and girls of high school age. Therefore, the school plant should be planned and equipped in such a way that the students will consider it the most desirable place in the community to learn, work and play.

FORM

That a well-balanced, effective program of education will accent communications among students in the classroom as well as communication between the teacher and the student group. Therefore, teaching areas should be designed to allow flexibility of seating arrangement. **(Note:** This is one of the most difficult jobs that the architect has: To provide a classroom in which, no matter where the student is seated, he will have proper seeing conditions and adequate natural ventilation.)

ECONOMY

That within each individual teaching area, such as Homemaking, English or Speech, there will always be changes in teaching techniques. Therefore, classrooms, laboratories and shops should be designed for economical and efficient adaptations to these changes.

TIME

That high school population will continue to grow and that courses of study will continue to be added to, or subtracted from, the curriculum. Therefore, the school must be designed so that it can be expanded economically and efficiently without marring the beauty of the school.

PROFESSIONAL ORGANIZATION OFFICES
Space Planning and Interior Design
Date of Project: Apr 1979

PROBLEM STATEMENTS

FUNCTION
Since the office is accessible to the general public during working hours, and since the office must be accessible to employees during evenings and weekends, **the design should resolve the inherent security requirements.**

Although the company seeks an identity as one firm through uniform spatial and finish standards, **the design should respond to the unique functional requirements of each department.**

Several types of people visit the office, each with unique circulation requirements: 1) employees, 2) clients, 3) recruits, 4) vendors; therefore, **the design should clearly separate conflicting circulation patterns.**

FORM
Since the company is a prestigious international organization, **the design should convey an appropriate and distinguished corporate image.**

Since the core elements in the building are arranged asymmetrically, **the space plan should resolve special layout requirements for elevator access, and for cross and vertical circulation.**

Since the company partners and managers are accustomed to the idea of hierarchy, **the design should maintain the arrangement of window offices.**

ECONOMY
Since the budget must remain within the corporate guidelines, **the design should emphasize areas of higher quality by "putting the money in public areas."**

Since the company has a substantial investment in existing finishes and furniture, **the design should reuse these items when appropriate.**

Since the company will expand incrementally over the next 10 years in the building, **the space plan should establish the most economical mix of finished and furnished spaces.**

TIME
The most economical leasing strategy requires some departments to switch floors at different time intervals; therefore, **the space plan should minimize disruption at each move, while considering the ultimate office arrangement.**

Since the exact growth of each department is uncertain, **the space plan should couple departments that might have offsetting growth patterns.**

Since the expansion strategy results in a very high utilization of available leased space, **the final phases may require a tighter efficiency to fit all the programmed area into three floors of the building.**

A TECHNICAL AND COMMUNITY COLLEGE
Master Plan
Date of Project: Apr 1972

PROBLEM STATEMENT

FUNCTION

The College actively seeks ways to increase service to the community. Some of the potentials for the new campus have been identified, e.g., library services, making space available for meetings, conferences, recitals, recreation, etc.; others will emerge. **This unusual outlook should be nourished and supported by a campus plan that is also "outward bound".**

FORM

The elongated, arched shape of the site, its undulating land form and the high contrast of cleared land versus dense woods create exceptional forces and **the campus plan must respond to these forces.**

Given the scale of other possible land developments in the surrounding area, the college will be relatively small in terms of conventional things which help to establish a strong identity (impressive building bulk or height, numbers of cars and people, visible activity, etc.). **Therefore, the planning should propose ways of developing a college identity that is competitive in its physical setting.**

ECONOMY

The college seeks a very high level of performance in return for its investment in services, plant and equipment and this attitude towards, or emphasis upon, **cost effectiveness should be intrinsic to the planning of the campus.**

TIME

The future will bring substantial change to the college; some of this can be anticipated in reasonable detail (enrollment growth, increases in certain instructional programs, etc.). Much of it, however, is obscure, especially those aspects of change and influence that will arise from the future development of this almost rural site area. **Therefore, the campus plan should respond to the certainty of change and its impreciseness by incorporating a very high quality of flexibility.**

It is uncertain whether the succeeding phases of planning and development of the campus will be performed in conventional ways or whether relatively new techniques of scheduling, managing and building will be employed; **therefore, the campus plan must be adaptable to both sets of processes.**

URBAN COMMUNITY COLLEGE
Schematic Design
Date of Project: Aug 1973

THE STATEMENT OF THE PROBLEM

FUNCTION
Since there is a diversity of student population and lifestyles, **there is the need to achieve a strong sense of place to foster interaction.**

Since the major user is the adult part-time student spending a short time in the facility, **careful consideration should be given to orientation and to circulation systems.**

Since the district has adopted an educational merchandising concept, **the visibility of the activities becomes a major design objective.**

Since the classrooms in the pool are shared by diverse teaching groups, **their physical distribution should be a major design determinant.**

FORM
Because of the diversity and transitory nature of the student body, **there is a need to develop a highly stimulating environment.**

Since there is a need for capturing the spirit of a new urban building type that combines educational, commercial and office activities, **design should respond to this unique need.**

Since the small urban site has numerous external physical and legal constraints, **the design should respond to these external influences as well as to the needs for functional requirements.**

ECONOMY
Since the budget establishes the quality of construction at "above average", **the design must consider the effect of urban conditions on materials and costs.**

TIME
Because of the indeterminancy of the academic programs now, and in the future, **convertibility and negotiability of classrooms should be a major design objective.**

OPERATIONAL
To meet the goal for September 1976 occupancy, unique scheduling techniques, efficient construction methods, timely decision-making in review and approvals, and availability of funds must be coordinated.

A PLANNED RECREATIONAL COMMUNITY
Master Plan
Date of Project: Oct 1973

PROBLEM STATEMENT

FUNCTION
Since the **fun park** will eventually be part of the development, **its influences should be taken into account while programming and planning the adjacent areas.**

Since the project has to be phased and different areas have different land uses, **an overall street hierarchy should be developed.**

FORM
Since the topography and the scale of development prevent a good sense of direction or orientation, **an overall informational and directional signage system should be developed.**

Since the Mary's Well area is an important and viable attraction for visitors and property owners, **the natural form of the area should be preserved.**

Since **water bodies** increase land value, **they should be preserved in as natural form as possible.**

Since open space is an element that occurs throughout the development, **the open space system should be utilized as a positive design element to enhance the total image.**

ECONOMY
Since the development depends on return on investment, **merchandising of features must consider short-term, as well as long-term, effects.**

TIME
Since the project development will be phased over the next five years, **the plan should respond to the phasing.**

UNIVERSITY RESEARCH PARK
Master and Capital Plan
Date of Project: Dec 1983

PROBLEM STATEMENTS

FUNCTION
Since ground tenant site area requirements are not yet known, **the master plan must be designed with a flexible lot subdivision system.**

FORM
Since there will be a public street right-of-way dividing the site, **the master plan design must integrate the two areas into a cohesive whole, as well as provide appropriate security for tenant sites.**

Since the site is relatively featureless, **the master plan design must provide the required image for the park.**

ECONOMY
Since the municipal improvement district will be developed in Phase One, **the master plan should allocate as much of site development to Phase One as feasible.**

TIME
Since the Park will be built in phases, **the master plan must locate the common support facilities and amenities to be able to serve all phases equally well.**

A COMMUNITY HOSPITAL
Schematic Design
Date of Project: Nov 1969

STATEMENT OF THE PROBLEM

FUNCTION
The whole hospital equals the strong functional interrelationship of highly individual functional departments.

Because the central service facility (dietary, laundry, storage) is located apart from the hospital, a unique service requirement must be met.

The essence of the hospital is the circulation of patients, staff and goods.

FORM
The climate and community attitudes will call for a regional architectural response.

The large, flat site will influence the form of the hospital towards a more horizontal development.

The hospital must project an open image to the community.

ECONOMY
Develop construction and distribution systems for people and goods that are both efficient and economical.

TIME
The hospital will have an unusually rapid growth pattern.

The departments will require a flexible plan with emphasis on expansibility and convertibility.

OPERATIONAL
Continuous growth without disturbing patient or total department activities will demand a form conducive to orderly growth and change.

COMMUNITY MENTAL HEALTH AND RETARDATION CENTER
Schematic Design
Date of Project: Mar 1969

STATEMENT OF THE PROBLEM

FUNCTION
Because of the importance of the functional duality of the Center as both a state and a community center for mental health and for mental retardation, **the solution should express this duality.**

Since the goal for coordinated service, training and research affects the multifunctional aspects, **the solution should encourage interdisciplinary mix between these aspects of mental health and mental retardation.**

Because the Center is a direct extension of the Psychiatric Institute and indirectly of other University health facilities, **the solution should provide a major pedestrian facility for staff and students to circulate between the University and the Center.**

Because of the psychological-sociological nature of the people of the community, **the solution should provide the user with a clear sense of orientation.**

FORM
Because of the relative position of the site to the University and the community, **the solution must provide for the interfacing of activities and of scale between the University and the immediate community.**

ECONOMY
Because of the community's interest in "economy of means" and because of the numerous functions to be provided within a low-to-medium unit cost of $30.46 sq. ft., **the solution should strive for economy and multi-use of space.**

TIME
Because the methods of mental health and mental retardation will change and because the needs of the community will change, **the Center must be adaptable to these changes.**

Because the facility will be used by the community on a continuing on-going basis, **the solution should capture the spirit of a 24-hour concourse.**

MEDICAL CENTER AND SCHOOL OF MEDICINE
Master Plan
Date of Project: Jul 1971

STATEMENT OF THE PROBLEM

FUNCTION
The School of Medicine has strong functional and administrative ties with the existing university campus; **hence, a physical and visual connection between the two campuses is important.**

Ambulant patient care is the dominant aspect of this medical education and **the character and positioning of the clinics must visibly reflect their key role.**

FORM
The Medical School educational and service programs are marked by their accessibility — health care for the walking patient as well as the acutely ill bed patient, extension services to the region, air transport for emergency care; **therefore, the school should have a corresponding sense of physical openness and outward orientation.**

Since there will be a large daily influx of patients at the clinics, many making their first visit, **special consideration must be made concerning patient, orientation and direction.**

Since the facility will house a variety of interrelated functions, **a key problem is to accommodate this functional mix while retaining some sense of order, orientation and location.**

The city is subject to severe dust storms, occasional snow and wide temperature swings, **so climate will be an important design factor, particularly of outdoor spaces.**

ECONOMY
Recognizing the severe limitations of the budget, **continue to use appropriate cost control techniques and seek creative expression of this "lean and clean" quality in the architecture.**

TIME
The Medical School will be the core of the future Medical Center; **therefore, the school must be able to evolve and to grow to meet these new responsibilities and affiliations.**

Medical education concepts and programs will continue to evolve; **therefore, the architecture must have the convertibility to accommodate change.**

MEDICAL CENTER AND SCHOOL OF MEDICINE

Schematic Design — First Phase
Date of Project: Aug 1972

STATEMENT OF THE PROBLEM

FUNCTION

The new facility must accommodate a variety of functions and traffic. **A key problem is to accommodate this mix, taking care to minimize the conflicts while accentuating the positive interactions necessary to medical education.**

In spite of the administrative division of the diagnostic and treatment services between the School of Medicine and the County Hospital, **the design must integrate these facilities into a coordinated workable unit serving both institutions.**

FORM

While the operational characteristics of the clinical and educational programs demand the extreme subdivision of space, **the overall design must permit the individual to maintain his orientation and to understand the building as a whole.**

The city is subject to severe dust storms, occasional snow and wide temperature swings, **climate will be an important design factor, particularly of outdoor spaces.**

ECONOMY

Recognizing the severe limitations of the budget, **continue to use appropriate cost control techniques and seek creative expression of this "lean and clean" quality in the architecture.**

TIME

Phase 1A is the initial increment in the long-range development of the University Medical Center; **therefore, the facilities must be able to accommodate the growth of major elements to achieve that goal without the interruption of medical and building services vital to the County Hospital and the School of Medicine.**

Medical education concepts and programs will continue to evolve; **therefore, the architecture must have the convertibility to accommodate change.**

OPERATIONAL

During the period between the occupancy of Phase 1A and the completion of the total Phase 1 facility, the School of Medicine will be conducting clinical, educational and administrative activities at three or more locations. **Therefore, special consideration should be given to the problems of patient orientation and transportation, the movement of staff supplies and records, and the economic utilization of resources by the dispersed activities.**

Because of the impact which the School of Medicine will have upon health care in the region, the scheduled completion and occupancy of the new facility is of prime importance. **The process must acknowledge the short schedule.**

RESEARCH AND DEVELOPMENT CENTER
Schematic Design
Date of Project: July 1984

PROBLEM STATEMENTS

FUNCTION
Since a high priority is placed on encouraging interaction between the research and office personnel, **the design should maximize the relationship between office and lab as an operating unit.**

Since there is no particular "typical division," **the site plan and building design should be based on a general model of a division, group and sector organization.**

FORM
Since the development of the adjacent land is unknown at this time, **it is important to control access to the connector road.**

Since the development of this site will serve as a model for future growth in the area, **the site should communicate that "this quality company leads in quality growth in a sensitive area."**

ECONOMY
Since this will be a corporate site, **building costs and site amenities should be consistent with those at other corporate sites.**

Since the company will own and operate these facilities, **the design should provide maximum opportunity for the owner/user to control the building systems and achieve low operating costs.**

Since energy efficient design is important, **those energy conservation measures which show a four year or better payback should be considered.**

TIME
Because the eventual occupants are not all identified, and because building usage will change over time, **the lab and office areas that comprise a "model division" should be flexible enough to accommodate smaller or larger operating units with a minimum of disruption.**

Since the project will be developed in pre-planned phases, **the project delivery strategy should allow for occupancy of Phase One facilities by May 1987, and for occupancy of Phase Two facilities by June 1989.**

OPERATIONAL
Because Phase Two construction will begin within months of the completion of Phase One, **the site design and phasing plan should locate Phase Two buildings to avoid serious construction obstructions to the users of the Phase One facilities.**

CONVENTION CENTER
Schematic Design
Date of Project: Dec 1968

PROBLEM DEFINITION

FUNCTION
The Convention Center includes an exhibit hall with meeting rooms, an arena and an auditorium. The facilities serve for convention functions and community use. Therefore, **the Center should function for a single occupancy by a large group or simultaneous occupancies by separate small groups.**

The presence of the Convention Center generates parking requirements for large numbers of vehicles. Therefore, **the Center should provide adequate parking facilities without restricting off-site traffic flow.**

The exhibit hall generates a requirement for large truck/tractor access to, and egress from, the site. Therefore, **the site must accommodate maneuvering and storage of truck/tractor units without interfering with off-site traffic flow.**

Since the Convention Center site is bounded by major through traffic arteries, **the new facilities should minimize the pedestrian-vehicle conflict.**

FORM
The Convention Center site is adjacent to waterfront property presently serving public use. Therefore, **the Center should be a good neighbor to the adjacent properties.**

Since the waterfront site is a unique feature of the city's image, **the Convention Center should touch the water and establish an activity connection at the water.**

Since the building site is adjacent to the water and has a poor solid condition for building, **the new facilities must tolerate severe storm conditions (high water, wave action, high winds) and must be structurally supported on deep piles.**

Since the Convention Center will be viewed from all sides, including "from the water", **the Convention Center should be handsome from all sides and from above.**

ECONOMY
The budget is adequate for good quality construction; however, **it is not without design implications.**

TIME
The present hotel capacity will have to expand to meet the ultimate requirements of the convention facilities (1500 to 2000 committed rooms). The success of the facilities depends on this expansion.

Phasing the building program will permit the interim time necessary for the business community response.

ADDITIONAL HEADQUARTERS OFFICE
Schematic Design
Date of Project: Oct 1984

PROBLEM STATEMENTS

FUNCTION
Since over thirty separate departments or organizational groups will be co-located on the same site, **the design should strive to maintain departmental identity while locating departments for more efficient interaction and communication.**

The number of automobiles on the site is projected to grow by over 150% by 1997. **On-site circulation and traffic to and from town will require careful and creative solutions to minimize traffic problems.**

Currently used workstation standards are a result of insufficient area available to house a growing population. Proposed space standards are larger. **The design should accommodate the larger standards through a phasing plan that upgrades areas incrementally as the population grows and expands in the new building.**

FORM
Since the new building will probably be in a more contemporary architectural style than the existing Headquarters, **the design should sensitively integrate a new facility that complements and does not clash with the existing structure.**

The existing and future facilities will share organizations and departments that will require constant interaction and movement. **Appropriate site location of the new building and some form of a connection between facilities are major design factors.**

The plan should maintain and reinforce the natural beauty of the site and the integrity of the formal entry by the careful placement of new facilities.

ECONOMY
Although the budget is adequate for a moderate quality level of construction, **prudent and judicious use of materials and systems that reinforce the solid image of the company is advised.**

TIME
Phased growth of the staff population between move-in 1987 and 1997 will provide for built-in expansion space in the early years. **The plan should recognize this and locate these expansion areas for maximum availability and flexibility.**

Growth of departments over time may mean relocation and movement both within and between buildings. **The design should recognize this and consider buffer areas that easily allow for departmental movement and interim usage of space.**

MANUFACTURING PLANT
Schematic Design
Date of Project: Nov 1980

PROBLEM STATEMENTS

FUNCTION
Since the operating center and team concepts lead to a strong and evolving organizational structure, **the design should respond with clear identity of areas and flexibility for change.**

Since safe and efficient traffic is a requirement, **the design must respond with a clear separation of pedestrian and vehicular traffic – and of car and truck movement.**

Since the production goals relate to layout efficiency, **the design must meet this criteria for efficiency.**

Since the program indicates different environmental conditions for machining and assembly, **the design should respond with a separation of these conditions.**

FORM
Since the partnership creates a totally new company, **the design should recognize the facility as a distinct corporate entity as well as a functioning manufacturing plant.**

Since the surrounding community is an important consideration, **the design must respond with enhancement of the environment through sensitive site development.**

ECONOMY
Since the type of construction is of moderate cost, **the design must proceed with rigorous cost control.**

TIME
Since the program indicates three potential stages of development, **the design must respond with strategies for growth.**

ENERGY
Since the manufacturing produces excess heat, **the design should take advantage of it when needed and dispose of it efficiently when it is not needed.**

CRIMINAL JUSTICE/YOUTH CENTER
Schematic Design
Date of Project: Jul 1975

PROBLEM STATEMENTS

FUNCTION
Since the living unit forms the background for the resident's identity and well-being, **the design must respond to a concept sensitive to this requirement.**

Since the functional organization calls for centralized service facilities surrounded by decentralized living units, **the design must respond to this grouping of activities.**

Since this is to be a medium security facility, **the design must include provisions for adequate supervision and control.**

FORM
Since the residents will be between the ages of 18 and 25, **the design must respond with a dynamic, playful, youthful character.**

Since the Environmental Impact Statement prescribes an image with a non-institutional character, **the design should respond with appropriate forms of a scale and proportion appropriate to satisfy this requirement.**

Since a normal, real world psychological environment is sought, **the design should respond with an atmosphere similar to a college campus.**

Since low cost of maintenance and adequate security are included in the requirements, **a high construction quality must be achieved.**

ECONOMY
Since the budget is adequate, but not luxurious, **the design must respond with simplicity and directness.**

TIME
Since expansion of the facility is uncertain, **the design should provide visual and functional unity at each stage of development.**

PERFORMING ARTS HALL
Schematic Design
Date of Project: Mar 1978

PROBLEM STATEMENTS

FUNCTION
Since all the performing arts need to be seen and heard under the best conditions, **the design should achieve superior sight lines and acoustical qualities.**

Since all the performing arts depend upon a direct communication between the performer and the audience, **the design should create an intimacy between the stage and the seating area.**

Since people like to see and to be seen, **the design of lobbies is an important part of a performing arts event.**

Since performing arts events occur primarily in the evening, **the design should emphasize the nature of night activity.**

Since convenient flow of sets, costumes and properties will reduce set-up and break-down time and costs, **the design should locate the stages at the same elevation as the receiving area, the scene shop and the loading dock.**

FORM
Since extraneous noise must be buffered from the performance area, **the design must acoustically isolate the mechanical room and scene shop.**

To reconcile the different seating capacity preferences of the performing arts in the large hall, **the design must provide simple mechanical/electrical technology to reduce the capacity from 2100 seats to 1400 seats.**

Since the Childrens' Theater will be a major tenant of the small hall, **the design must pay special attention to sight line and seating arrangement requirements for children.**

ECONOMY
Since the large hall must accommodate symphony, opera and ballet, **the multi-purpose stage design must reconcile the different requirements of these arts.**

Since the small hall must accommodate a variety of performances in addition to Childrens' Theater, **the modified thrust stage must be designed to be multi-purpose.**

Since the cost for the architectural fabric of the large hall has been established within an excellent to grand quality, **the design should respond accordingly.**

TIME
Because change is inevitable, **the concept of convertibility is important, particularly in offices for organizations and in the large hall (multi-form).**

Programming Procedures

There is a direct relationship between the Information Index and the Programming Procedures listed in this section. The Information Index* uses key and evocative words and phrases to trigger specific questions about the project. The programming procedures give meaning to those words—charging them with meaning so that thereafter the words evoke questions beyond any prepared checklist.

These programming procedures are intended to provide stimulus to the programming process. There are more than enough procedures here to get the project under way. Certain procedures may apply in a specific project while others may not; but you'll have to test them to find out. You should then generate other procedures which apply to the specific project—still keeping the whole problem in mind.

*Page 36

Establish Goals

Function

(1)   Understand why the project is being undertaken.

(2)   Investigate policy concerning maximum number of people to be accommodated.

(3)   Identify goals to maintain sense of individual identity within large mass of people.

(4)   Identify goals for degrees and types of privacy and for group interaction.

(5)   Identify goals concerning the promotion of human values.

(6)   Investigate the hierarchy of values of the client/user if hierarchy of goals is not explicit.

(7)   Identify goals concerning the promotion of certain activities as prime interests and their quality level.

(8)   Identify goal concerning the priority of relationships.

(9)   Identify goal concerned with the types of security required.

(10) Identify goal toward the effective continuity of progression (flow) of people and things.

(11) Investigate policies concerning the segregation of people, vehicles and things.

(12) Identify goals dealing with the promotion of chance and planned encounters.

(13) Understand the implications of a goal for functional efficiency.

(14) Identify policy regarding transportation (parking).

Form

(15) Identify any client attitudes toward existing elements on the site (trees, water, open space, facilities, utilities).

(16) Identify client attitudes toward the facility response to its environment.

(17) Investigate land use policy for efficiency and environmental character.

(18) Identify policies concerning coincident planning and relations with the neighboring community.

(19) Identify policies concerning the investment in, or improvement of, the neighboring community.

(20) Identify client attitudes toward the psychological environment to be provided.

(21) Identify goals concerned with the promotion of personal individuality of the user.

(22) Identify goals dealing with the flow of people and vehicles to provide a psychological environment with a sense of orientation (knowing where you are), or a sense of entry (knowing where to enter).

(23) Identify the image which must be projected.

(24) Identify client attitude toward the quality of the physical environment.

(25) Identify client expectations of the balance of space and quality.

Economy

(26) Identify the extent of available funds.

(27) Investigate goal for cost effectiveness.

(28) Investigate goal for maximum return...the most for the money.

(29) Investigate goal for return on investment...for achieving financial gain.

(30) Identify goal for minimizing operational costs of the physical plant.

(31) Identify goal for minimizing maintenance and operating costs.

(32) Identify goal establishing a priority on life cycle costs or initial costs.

Time

(33) Identify client attitude toward historic preservation.

(34) Determine client attitude toward being static or dynamic as a social or functional organization.

(35) Identify client attitude toward anticipated change.

(36) Identify client expectations for growth.

(37) Identify the desired occupancy date.

Collect and Analyze Facts

Function

(38) Process raw statistical data into useful information.

(39) Generate area parameters from general activities (Ex. 150 sq. ft. per office worker).

(40) Organize the manpower schedule listing the number of persons in each category and possibly their workloads.

(41) Analyze the physical, social, emotional and intellectual characteristics of the people to be served.

(42) Analyze the characteristics of the community involved.

(43) Evaluate the potential loss to determine the degree of security controls required.

(44) Study the time-distance movement requirements.

(45) Analyze the different kinds of traffic lanes required by building occupants, pedestrians and vehicles.

(46) Analyze the behavioral patterns of the client/user.

(47) Evaluate the space adequacy for the number of people and their activities to be housed.

(48) Analyze the requirements of special groups of people...such as the handicapped.

Form

(49) Analyze the existing site conditions to include: contours, views, natural features, buildable areas, access and egress, utilities, size and capacity.

(50) Analyze the climate to include climatalogical data on seasonal temperatures, precipitation, snow, sun angles and wind direction.

(51) Evaluate the form-giving significance of code and zoning requirements.

(52) Evaluate the soil test report and determine the implications on cost and design.

(53) Evaluate the floor area ratio, the ground area coverage, people per acre and other comparative measures of density.

(54) Analyze local materials and the immediate surroundings of the site for possible influences.

(55) Understand the psychological implications of form on territoriality.

(56) Understand the psychological implications of form on the movement of people and vehicles.

(57) Establish mutual understanding of building quality on a quantitative basis (cost per square foot).

(58) Understand the effect of building efficiency (commonly referred as net to gross ratio) on quality.

(59) Establish the adequacy of functional support spaces (such as assigned storage) as an indication of quality.

Economy

(60) Establish cost per square foot considering escalation factor, local cost index and construction quality level.

(61) Establish on a trial-run the maximum budget required.

(62) Analyze the time-use factors for the different functions tentatively considered for combination.

(63) Evaluate the market analysis report and determine the implications on design.

(64) Analyze the different costs for the alternative energy sources.

(65) Analyze the climate factors, the wear and tear level of activities and their implications on building materials.

(66) Analyze economic data related to initial versus life cycle costs.

Time

(67) Establish the full significance of the existing building as having historic, aesthetic and/or sentimental values.

(68) Evaluate the historical significance of neighboring buildings.

(69) Generate space parameters from specific activities and the number of participants (Ex. 15 sq. ft. per dining seat).

(70) Identify the existing activities most likely to change.

(71) Identify long term functional projections indicating growth or no growth.

(72) Determine a realistic time schedule for the total project delivery.

Uncover and Test Concepts

Function

(73) Test the many services as best being centralized or decentralized.

(74) Uncover concepts derived from the physical, social and emotional character-istics of people...as individuals, in small groups, in large groups.

(75) Investigate the sizes and kinds of groups to be housed—both now and in the future.

(76) Understand the client's need for hu-manistically sized groups.

(77) Uncover the need for a family of closely related activities to be integrated into a unit.

(78) Uncover the need for privacy (audio and/or visual) and for the degree of privacy (minimum, maximum) requiring isolation.

(79) Uncover concepts establishing an order of importance, a priority based on what is valued or preferred and affecting relative position, sizes and quality.

(80) Understand how security controls are used to protect property and control personnel movement.

(81) Evaluate the flow-charts dealing with the movement of people, vehicles, services, goods and information.

(82) Identify the need to completely separate traffic lanes to segregate different kinds of people (prisoners and public), different kinds of vehicular traffic (campus and urban traffic) or pedestrian and vehicular traffic.

(83) Identify the need for a common space dedicated to multi-directional, multi-purpose traffic and intended to pro-mote change and planned encounters.

(84) Understand the organizational concepts and the functional relationships.

Form

(85) Evaluate the natural features of the site and identify those to be preserved or enhanced.

(86) Evaluate the climate analysis and determine the implications on climate controls.

(87) Evaluate the form-giving implications of the code survey and identify the salient safety precautions.

(88) Evaluate the soil analysis report and determine the possibility of special foundations and their costs.

(89) Evaluate climate, demographic data, site conditions, and land value to establish general density standards.

(90) Evaluate policy concerning the neighboring community to uncover the concept of sharing or interdependence.

(91) Uncover the need for an individual's home base or territoriality.

(92) Uncover the need for good orientation...maintaining a sense of direction through a building or campus.

(93) Uncover the need for the concept of accessibility which promotes a sense of entrance and of arrival...providing direct access to public-oriented facilities.

(94) Uncover the general character of architectural form which the client intends to project as an image.

(95) Understand that quality control is an operational concept used to provide the highest quality level feasible after the balance of quality/cost factors.

(96) Relate the project to the quality of its surroundings and to its function.

(97) Expose the client's preconceived solutions as a basis for analysis and discussion.

Economy

(98) Understand that cost control is an operational concept used to provide a realistic preview of probable costs after evaluating the pertinent facts.

(99) Understand that the efficient allocation of funds is an operational concept which utilizes formulas for impartial allocation of space and money.

(100) Evaluate the time-use factors to determine the feasibility of combining various functions into a multi-function space.

(101) Uncover the need for the concept of merchandising used to promote business activities.

(102) Test the concept of energy conservation to determine the design and cost implications.

Time

(103) Uncover the concept of adaptability in recycling an historic building for new activities and functions.

(104) Test the concept of tailored precision versus loose fit, in determining the area requirements for an organization which might be static or dynamic.

(105) Uncover the concept of convertibility used to provide for interior changes in a building to accommodate future changes in activities.

(106) Uncover the concept of expansibility used to provide for exterior wall changes in a building to accommodate future growth.

(107) Test the conventional and fast-track procedures against the occupancy date to determine a realistic time schedule.

Determine Needs

Function

(108) Establish the space requirements for each activity.

(109) Establish parking and outdoor area requirements.

(110) Evaluate the building efficiency ratio which was used to determine gross area requirements.

(111) Understand the cost implications of functional alternatives.

Form

(112) Establish mutual agreement with client on the construction quality expressed as cost per square foot.

(113) Consider the factors of the physical and psychological environment as well as site conditions as influences on the construction budget.

Economy

(114) Analyze the cost estimate and test for comprehensiveness and realism...leaving no doubt as to what comprises the total budget required.

(115) Establish a balance between space requirements, the budget and quality.

(116) Evaluate the energy budget (if required).

(117) Evaluate outline on operating costs (if required).

(118) Evaluate report on life cycle costs (if required).

Time

(119) Consider phasing of construction as an alternative if the project proved unfeasible in the initial analysis.

(120) Evaluate the realism of the escalation factor to cover the time lag between programming and mid-construction.

State the Problem

Function

(121) State the unique performance requirements to satisfy the personal or popular needs of the client/user.

(122) State the unique performance requirements to accommodate the major activities in the project.

(123) State the unique performance requirements created by the relationship among activities in the project.

Form

(124) Identify and abstract the major form giving influences of the site on the building design.

(125) Identify the salient environmental influences on the building design.

(126) Identify the quality of the project and its implications on the building design.

Economy

(127) Establish an attitude toward the initial budget and its influence on the fabric and geometry of the building.

(128) Determine if operating costs are critical issues and establish a design directive.

(129) Reconcile the possible difference between the initial budget and life cycle costs.

Time

(130) Consider the possible influences of historic surroundings.

(131) Consider which major activities will most likely remain static and fixed and which might be dynamic and flexible.

(132) Consider the implications of change and growth on long range performance.

Sophistication, Situations, Simplification

There are different programming methods with many variations, and there are different levels of sophistication within each method which reflect the increasing complexity of building projects. Note that the four levels described in this section each build on the experience of the previous level and on the basic principles and elementary techniques of the first level.

There is a close relationship between the levels of programming and the variable conditions under which services must be provided. This section implies that a beginner in programming must learn to make adjustments and modifications without having to invent a new method.

A beginner in programming must also learn not to be perplexed by the complexity of a project. This section describes how the programming process, the considerations and client decisions can bring order and simplification to any design problem.

Four Levels of Programming

The development of programming within this method (separating programming from design) has been cumulative through four levels of sophistication. This development is the result of many years in the professional field, working with clients in a wide variety of situations. The identification of the four levels is empirical and well-tested.

The problem seeking approach involving the five-step process and four basic considerations is applicable to all four levels. In the fourth level, the four basic considerations are expanded to five to include the political considerations in urban problems.

The four levels of sophistication might best be described and understood through the following factors:

(1) Analytical techniques applied

(2) The scope of management services and the programming team

(3) The changing nature of problems

(4) The object of research

(5) Client structure and decision-making

(6) User involvement

First Level

First level programming consists largely of the traditional architectural services in which the architect merely organizes the information received from the client, adds the information on the site analysis and tests the simple economic feasibility of the project. The information is sufficient to formulate the statement of the problem.

The two-phase process provides the appropriate information for the two phases of the design process: schematic design and design development. First generation programming leads to the design of a simple, perhaps single, building—usually a familiar building type.

If the programmer is inexperienced in the client's building type, he needs to obtain a background through library research, a survey of similar projects, etc. This background will improve his communication with the client and his understanding of the nature of the problem.

Decision-making is centralized in the client owner who is also the user. The client is an active, working member of the team.

Second Level

The expanded scope of second level programming has introduced the computer as an analytical tool to reinforce the architect in problem seeking. Computer applications have also been found useful in subsequent levels. Some early computer applications include:

(1) Generating space requirements

(2) Manipulating the space inventory

(3) Analyzing functional affinities

(4) Sophisticated economic analysis

The two-phase may become a three-phase process on projects which require a master planning phase as well as schematic design and design development phases. The idea of providing the appropriate information for each phase still applies.

In second level programming, the architect begins to provide consulting services to lead the client through the decision-making process. The architect takes the leadership to develop the program, provides most of the information through extensive interviewing, statistical analysis and long-range projections.

Goal setting and the resolution of conflicting values is a time consuming, but extremely important, aspect of programming at this level. This had best be left to the professional who has the experience in the building type and the social and political awareness to communicate effectively with the complex client organization.

Second level programming deals with a complex building group. The architect must be "specialized" in the building type with extensive experience as a background for space parameters and workloads. His experience will be useful in testing functional and organizational relationships and concepts and in understanding the implications of the organizational structure.

The programming team becomes more interdisciplinary. Specialists are needed to deal with problems in analysis, and with complex functional organizational requirements.

The client is still the final authority in decision making. Characteristically, the client in this level is a multi-headed group in which the owner is not necessarily the user. The user group may be comprised of several groups with conflicting interests.

Third Level

At this level, programming is still aimed at facilities design; however, there are generally many issues that must be resolved before a facilities program can be developed. The analysis includes a survey of existing operational and functional plans dealing with the management activities concerned with efficient operation and the social and functional organization of an institution or organization.

The management of the team becomes a major aspect at this level—the organization of work, the logistics of trips, the preparation of presentation material, and the timing of critical decisions to permit work to progress without recycling.

This level deals with extremely large, mixed use projects such as an entire industrial community, a military community or a university city. The projects involve a full spectrum of building types within a comprehensive master plan. This level of programming will probably remain the exclusive domain of the large, highly specialized practice of multi-company joint venture organizations.

The program development requires an extensive background of experience from a variety of consultants and volumes of detailed documentation to justify and support every decision and recommendation made by the architect and the consultants.

One important characteristic of programming at this level (beyond size of project) is the total leadership of the architect to develop the program without the involvement of the client organization, or with minimum involvement at best.

There is likely to be a very complex administrative organization between the client owner and the architect which processes approvals. Yet, high level decisions tend to be autocratic, whether by corporation presidents or governmental executives. The user group may, or may not, be available to the process. Still, the architect has to create a model of the user organization and a profile of the characteristics of the user.

Fourth Level

This level is involved with urban problems and, therefore, the major considerations of function, form, economy and time are expanded to include the political consideration. Involvement by the architect/planning consultant is at the bureaucratic level where planning problems are comingled with political issues and power struggles.

Fourth level programming deals with a whole series of loosely connected problems in urban development. These problems are not always facilities oriented.

Typical of these problems might be publicly financed projects in which the planning and design of facilities is a secondary issue to the larger issues of land location and use, financing and public acceptance.

Research must be extensive enough for the recommendations to withstand public scrutiny. The architect/planner who wishes to serve in this environment must cope with all of the issues surrounding the project. He must seek alternatives and strategies.

This level of programming is an area for firms of all sizes involving all types of publicly funded building projects and for architects with a strong sense of public service and a high tolerance for the bureaucratic process.

The Information Index is expanded to accommodate political motivation. This should indicate that decision making may put all logic aside for public image and expediency. The structure of this complex client would indicate more conflicting values, longer funding schedules and public presentations involving advocacy groups and bureaucratic organizations.

Summary

The following summary makes use of key phrases to describe the four levels. It may be clear that essentially the different levels depend on the levels of complexity of the problems and the client structure, and on the team and services required to deal with them.

First Level

Two-phase process
Traditional services
Simple, single building
Familiar building type
Background research to help communication
Simple client structure
Centralized decision-making
Client Owner/User involvement

Second Level

Two or three phase process
Consulting services
Building type specialists
Interdisciplinary team
Complex client organization
Multi-head client decisions
Conflicting user groups

Third Level

Three phase process
Pre-programming surveys
Extensive project management
Wide variety of consultants
Multi-company specialists
Joint venture organization
Extremely large, mixed use projects
Research to provide documented justification
   for recommendations
Complex administrative organization processes
   client approvals
Autocratic high level decisions
Non-participating user group

Fourth Level

Considerations expanded to include political
   considerations
Bureaucratic process
Small, large firms with sense of public service
Urban development problems
Research to withstand public scrutiny
Complex client structure
Political decision-making
Advocacy groups

Variable Conditions

In approaching a project, the programmer must be able to identify those conditions which will determine the scope of programming services required as well as the techniques to be used. Different situations call for different responses. The following list might help to identify those conditions:

Client Information

The client is part of the team. The information is generated by the client. They are his goals, his ideas, his needs, his land, his money. However, it makes a difference whether the information is handed to the programmer by the client and his consultant or whether the information is generated by the client and the programmer.

In the first instance, the information is likely to be incomplete; few consultants would provide site and budget analyses. Even fewer would provide a reasonable building efficiency. In the second instance, it is the programmer's responsibility to see that the information is complete and predictively reasonable.

Two or Three Phase Process

It makes a difference if the programming is in two phases (1) for schematic design and (2) for design development; or if programming is in three phases (1) for master planning, (2) for schematic design and (3) for design development.

It's a matter of level of details. Programming for master planning can be based on crude figures and rough information which must be refined for schematic design and further refined for design development. It's like going from a reducing glass to a magnifying glass.

The sources of information vary: Board of Trustees' policies for master planning, management decisions for schematic design and user requirements for design development.

Conventional or Concurrent Scheduling

It makes a difference if the process is on a conventional schedule or on a concurrent schedule.

Concurrent scheduling (known as fast-track) requires that some decisions be made sooner, that the money be locked in earlier, that the space program be looser and that the predictive parameters be shorter and more general. The overall amount of time in programming is the same as for conventional scheduling but, for concurrent scheduling, the initial programming period is shorter and requires more experienced programmers.

Conventional or Systems Building

It makes a difference if the techniques include conventional means or a systems building technique. But this is true: Once you consider systems building techniques, you might also consider concurrent scheduling procedures.

The tendency is to program a systems building with a definite module in mind—making space requirements more precise. However, this precision is lost among the general space requirements in concurrent scheduling. The issue of mechanical systems must be resolved earlier: rooftop units versus conventional units.

Available Funds

It makes a difference if there is a fixed limit to the client's available funds or if the budget is open-ended or undetermined.

Every client's budget has a limit. Sooner or later this limit becomes evident. An open-ended budget implies carte blanche freedom; however, it merely postpones the balancing of the budget. In either case, an early trial run cost estimate can be used to advantage in approximating the inevitable fixed budget.

Predicting Cost and Quality

It makes a difference if the cost and quality of construction is based on general experience (cost, location, time, quality) such as $30/sq. ft., $50/sq. ft. or $100/sq. ft. or, if these are dependent upon a special selection of specific materials perhaps refined at a later date, breaking unit costs into subsystems.

Since the selection of specific materials involves design decisions, the selection rarely occurs in programming but, when it does, the result is more precise and more time-consuming.

Building Type

It makes a difference if the building type has unique requirements, such as a nuclear science center might have had in 1958, or if it is a familiar building type.

With a familiar type, it is possible to use space parameters derived from past experience. With a unique type, the programmer is more dependent on the user for space parameters.

Efficiency vs Human Values

It makes a difference if the conditions emphasize optimum efficiency or compromised logic toward human values.

Regardless of the emphasis on efficiency, it is the architect's responsibility to test the conditions for human values.

Economy vs Performance

It makes a difference if the emphasis is on economic modeling or on performance requirements.

Regardless of the emphasis on economic modeling, the architect must test for the quality and quantity of space.

Anticipating Change

It makes a difference if the conditions call for tight tailored requirements or loose fit requirements.

In the first instance, the building will work well initially and, thereafter, it must be altered to fit changing conditions. In the second instance, the building works in a spacious fashion but the loose fit postpones initial alterations.

Client Composition

It makes a difference if the client is essentially one person or a group of persons.

A large client group requires special communication techniques that will promote general understanding.

Client Decision Making

It makes a difference if the decision making is centralized or decentralized.

When the decision making is decentralized, the programmer faces his most serious challenge to reconcile the different points of view through documentation and graphic analysis techniques. When the decision making is centralized, the programmer must seek out the decision maker and interview him as early as possible. An important decision maker may be protected by a large staff from such interviews; yet, the staff may easily misread his intentions.

Project Organization

It makes a difference if the project is organized in the traditional manner—client/architect/contractor—or if the project is organized differently, as a project under construction management.

Role playing is even more important in an innovative project organization—to prevent chaos—since decisions are made out of the traditional sequence. For example, construction decisions may be made early during the programming of a project under the management of a construction management firm.

Client Attitude

It makes a difference if the client is rational and systems oriented or if he's irrational and solution oriented.

When a client is irrational, the information needs to be recycled periodically to test it for validity. This client does not want to see the analysis but merely the results of analysis. The architect must go through the analytical phase privately to preserve his own sanity...his own reason.

Client Participation

It makes a difference if the client is willing to participate in the programming process or if the client relies on the programmer and on consultants for specific proposals or recommendations.

The client's reliance on proposals and recommendations places a heavy responsibility on the programmer and on consultants to do research and comparative analyses to justify each recommendation.

How to Simplify Design Problems

Some architectural design problems are quite simple and familiar. They are easy to manage. On the other hand, there are those architectural design problems which are indeed complex and unique. These problems must be simplified and clarified before they become manageable.

There is no need to panic; start in an organized manner. Use the Information Index, or just the basic framework of steps and considerations. If you start with the recommended method of inquiry—the five step process—you won't lose time thrashing aimlessly. You'll know what the end product will be: the statement of the problem.

And it is when the problem is complex and unique that analysis is really effective in clarification. Use the four considerations as the major classifications of information; they are the components of the whole problem.

Clients must be stimulated intellectually to make sound decisions at the right time. Sound decisions are needed to simplify the problem.

Undoubtedly there are many ways to make a design problem manageable. Good communication techniques and graphic analysis certainly help. However, take a look at the three ways which follow and note how they might help to simplify a design problem.

1. Use the Five-Step Process

a. To collect information and determine its validity—separating fact from fantasy by identifying the inter-relationships of information in the different steps.

b. To spot pertinent information—by testing goals and concepts for design implications that might qualify them as part of the design problem.

c. To process voluminous facts into useful concise information—by determining the bare implications of data, what it means.

d. To analyze a client's preconceived solution, to pinpoint the actual requirement—by tracing the solution back to a programmatic concept and even back to a goal.

e. To focus on information critical to schematic design—by filtering out information more appropriate to routine engineering or to design development.

f. To distinguish major concepts from minor details — going from the general to the particular.

g. To organize the information for cooperative evaluation, consensus and decision-making—to be able to trace the resultant Needs back to Goals, Facts and Concepts.

h. To lead to a clear statement of the

problem—by seeking the essence, recognizing the obvious, and discovering the uniqueness of the problem.

i. To guide individual members of the project team toward a unified effort.

2. Use the Four Major Considerations and Their Sub-Categories.

a. To search for enough information to provide a clear, well rounded perception.

b. To classify the wide range of factors which constitute the whole problem.

c. To concentrate on the whole problem without excluding the major factors.

d. To analyze the whole problem—to identify the sub-categories as sub-problems and to understand their inter-relationships.

e. To analyze the sub-problems separately within the limits of their inter-relationships.

f. To focus on the elements of an architectural design problem as opposed to some other kind of problem outside the grasp of control.

3. Stimulate Client Decision-Making

a. To establish the program requirements.

b. To reduce the number of unknowns.

c. To provide more complete information.

d. To limit the number of alternative design solutions to those responding to the design problem.

Useful Techniques

Information is a basic element in programming. Facts and ideas, conditions and decisions, statistics and estimates–all these and many more comprise the information needs. This section emphasizes communication techniques–how to facilitate the transfer of information. The transfer is best explained in the context of a typical programming schedule which features the squatters technique. This section involves feedback and feedforward of information. It also covers the use of automated techniques in processing data into information. The section ends with a technique to evaluate the programming package of information and a technique for building evaluation.

Typical Programming Schedule

The typical programming schedule described here is appropriate for medium-sized projects. Small and large-sized projects would require adjustments in this typical schedule. Each project schedule involves management decisions which will determine how concurrent or how sequential the operational activities might be. In order that these activities be understood more clearly, they have been listed in a logical sequence as follows:

A. **Project Initiation**

1. Office organization

   a. organize project team

   b. prepare work plan

   c. prepare list of data needs

2. Organizational meeting with client owner/manager

   a. to identify decision makers

   b. to elicit the initial set of goals from owner/top management

   c. to schedule client/user for programming squatters

   d. to obtain data from existing records

   e. to obtain capacity/staff requirements

   f. to obtain site survey and soils analysis

   g. to obtain plans of existing facilities

   h. to arrange for distribution of questionnaire to users

B. **Concurrent Activities**

1. Conduct site analysis

2. Tour existing and/or similar facilities

3. Have client/manager prepare schedule for squatters week interviews

4. Arrange through the client/manager for a squatters workroom near the users and the site

5. Collect user questionnaires

C. **Office Preparation**

1. Research building type/client

2. Research cost data and area parameters

3. Process and tabulate users' questionnaire

4. Analysis of data received from client

5. Prepare wall display:

   a. present initial space requirements on "brown sheets" (refer to page 165)

   b. draw initial analysis cards (refer to page 170)

6. Prepare squatters interview questions

D. **Programming Squatters**

1. Set up the workroom and wall display

2. Hold kick-off meeting with users as a group

   a. to explain approach

   b. to explain what interviewer needs to know and by when

3. Main body of interviews

   a. with client/user groups

      (1) to collect specific data

      (2) to test documented information on wall display

      (3) to plan for next level of detail

   b. with client owner/management

      (1) to confirm previous data

      (2) to reveal new data

4. Conduct work sessions

   a. to report the implications of information to client for confirmation

   b. to identify conflicts needing reconciliation

   c. to identify issues yet to be resolved

   d. to test the feasibility of the project

      (1) to balance the total budget with the space requirements and the quality of construction

      (2) to consider alternatives which result in a balanced budget

   e. to make final revisions

5. Hold wrap-up meeting with client/owner and users as a group

    a. to present the wall display resulting from the week's activities

    b. to receive informal approval of the program

6. Clean up the workroom and pack up to go back to the office

E. Program Documentation

1. Follow standard outline (refer to page 180)

2. Photocopy and reduce analysis cards for draft program

3. Submit draft program to client for formal approval

F. Approval and Hand-Off

1. Receive client review comments

2. Obtain client approval of program

3. Correct wall display and report

4. Present wall display to design team

5. Write problem statements with designers

6. Reprint and distribute final report

Typical Programming Schedule

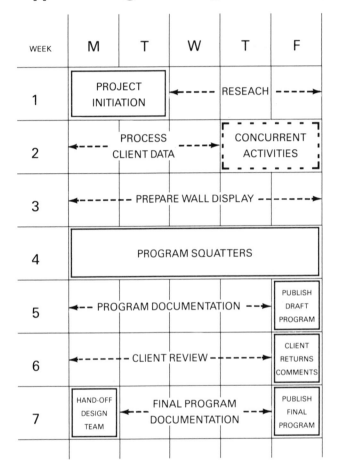

Project Initiation

Before meeting with the client for the first time, the project team is organized and the tasks are assigned. The team may consist of a lead programmer, an assistant programmer, a project manager, and sometimes a specialist for a particular building type. A work plan is prepared to include a tentative time schedule. And a list is prepared of the initial data needed from the client.

The project team goes to the client's premises for an organization meeting. One of the main reasons for the meeting is to identify the decision makers. It can be assumed that those people who have the responsibility and accountability for the product have the authority for decision making. The client/owner is usually identified as the main decision maker; however, the client/user and governmental agencies influence decisions.

Since project goals can determine the nature of the data to be gathered, it is prudent to elicit an initial set of goals from the owner and top management – before they get down to details. The programming process is explained and the time schedule is reviewed.

This is the time to obtain data from existing records and to obtain the project's maximum capacity and the staff requirements. If this data is not immediately available, then it must be mailed as soon as possible. The project manager seeks to obtain the site survey and the soils analysis, as well as plans of the existing facilities.

Once the client/manager has been designated, he is asked to make the distribution of the questionnaire to the users with instructions for their return at a certain time. The questionnaire serves to identify the type of information and the level of detail to be discussed at the interview.

Concurrent Activities

Several concurrent activities need to take place sometime during the second week: the site analysis, the tour of existing or similar facilities, and the work of the client/manager. He assigns a workroom, selects the users to be interviewed, and prepares a schedule for the interviews during the squatters week.

Office Preparation

Back at the office, the programmers research the pertinent building type, user characteristics, and area parameters. They contact cost estimators for cost data at various construction quality levels.

When the users' questionnaires are received, they are processed and tabulated. All the data received from the client is analyzed and interpreted into useful information. It is organized and classified through the use of the information index.

It usually takes five working days to prepare the wall display. The initial space requirements are documented graphically on brown sheets and a skeletal set of analysis cards are drawn around the initial goals, researched facts, and obvious concepts. A review of the information index will indicate missing information and questions to be asked during the squatters interviews. A trial run on balancing the total budget is useful at this time.

Programming Squatters

The squatters technique was developed to solve a communication problem with clients at a long distance from the office. Setting up an "office," practically in view of the site and on the client's premises, is certainly a good solution. The users and the owners are easily available for interaction and decision making. Working efficiency is achieved by isolating the team members from the office telephone and other projects. In this way they can concentrate on the task at hand.

Programming Squatters Agenda

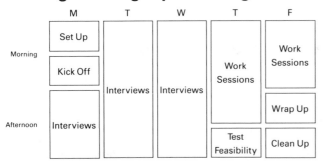

A programming squatters follows a well thought out agenda. It begins on Monday morning with setting up the workroom. The most important feature of the workroom is plenty of wall space for pinning up displays.

An early kick-off meeting is held for all participants as a group. This session involves an explanation of the programming process, the schedule of activities, and an overview of the status of the project at that time. The participants are told what the interviewer needs to know and by when.

A programming squatters proceeds through Wednesday with interviews of individual client/user groups. Most interviews can be accomplished within a period of one hour. The schedule should provide an hour's break between interviews to allow the transcription of rough notes to analysis cards. Each user group reviews their previously submitted "want list" and modifies it realistically on the brown sheets. The interviews are used to further clarify the responses to the questionnaire and to confirm the programmer's conclusions.

Using the information index, the interviewer can pursue the uncovering of new data. Here he must act as a catalyst for decision making. He may present alternatives or evaluate gains and risks to stimulate a decision. Details concerning minor equipment are documented, but postponed for use in design development.

The client user group might emphasize specific objectives and functional relationships, as well as the physical and psychological environment.

It is concerned with its needs, knowing how these needs will be met, and with occupying and testing the finished building.

Interviews with the client/owner and management staff are a good source for project and operational goals and overall concepts. This group is concerned with organization, finances, and change, with cost and quality control.

Interviews depend on the amount and kind of client participation. With or without interviews, it is difficult to avoid work sessions. On Thursday, the programmers consolidate and display all the information reviewed over the past three days. The display of information may take the form of feedback to the client. In effect, the display indicates what the programmer perceives to be the important and pertinent information. The programmer then asks the client for confirmation and for decisions in the case of conflicting information. Or he may identify issues and ask for their resolution.

But the most critical function of the work sessions is to balance the total budget with the space requirements and the quality of construction. Graphic analysis cards and brown sheets are used as working tools to determine the space program and to balance the budget. A preliminary cost estimate analysis is presented toward the end of Thursday to key client decision makers, which should determine the project feasibility.

Often the user requests (the wants) are more than are possible within the budget. It is important, then, to set priorities, to consider alternatives, and to make decisions about the project scope. After this session, it may be necessary to meet again with the individual groups to adjust the requirements. Friday morning is reserved for this purpose and for preparing the final presentation.

Early Friday afternoon, the wrap-up presentation is made to all participants as a group and a preliminary approval of the program as it stands is requested. The squatters week ends with the cleaning of the workroom and packing to go back to the office.

Program Documentation

The report for formal approval need not be more than photocopy reductions of the analysis cards and brown sheets together with enough text to explain the total program. This could be done within a standard report outline based on the programming steps. (Refer to page 180.) This draft program is submitted to the client for review and formal approval.

Approval and Hand-Off

With such intensive client participation, formal approval is not difficult. The client's review comments are incorporated into the wall display and into the report. It is essential to present the wall display to the design team since the information is usually encoded. The graphic analysis and the concise nature of the program, together with the verbal presentation, make it possible for the design team to assimilate what would have been a complex program.

The programmer then helps the designer to state the problem by flagging the information he perceives to be a potential form-giver.

The statement of the problem is added to the wall display and to the final report. It remains to reprint and distribute the final report to the client and the design team members. However, it is the wall display, and not the bound report, that communicates the information to the design team.

The design team then prepares to go on a design squatters, but that is not covered in this book.

Questionnaires

The use of questionnaires can be a valid method of gathering data before the programming squatters. Questionnaires can be an integral part of background research; however, they can provide only a part of the data required for a successful project. The extent of their value must be understood and they must be used judiciously and intelligently. To be successful data gathering tools, questionnaires must be well thought out, consciously and carefully designed for a specific audience, and aimed like a rifle shot, not broadcast like a shotgun blast.

A questionnaire or survey form is often the first impression an architect makes on his client and the facility users. Since questionnaires can help or hurt the architect's reputation in the client's eyes, they must be designed and used carefully.

The following guidelines concerning the design, usage, value and problems of questionnaires should be considered.

Design

Determine the data that is needed and the best way to get it.

Ask these questions:
What is needed?
Who probably has it?
How should the question be asked and answered?
What is the best vehicle for asking it?

Consider two or more questionnaires: one for executives (broad, strategic, qualitative), and one for users (focused, operational, functional, quantitative).

Customize each questionnaire to gather the right data from the right people.

Strive for legibility, clarity, simplicity.

Use filled-in sample responses–include examples of the types of responses.

Provide clear directions—do not assume the reader has done this before.

Create the shortest and most specific form possible—people are busy and your questionnaire is just one more unscheduled task for them.

Make the form interesting and graphic—attract and keep your readers' attention.

Provide enough space for responses/answers.

Lastly, trial-run the newly designed questionnaire—test it with colleagues before you distribute it.

Use

Realize early that questionnaires are not **always** appropriate.

Provide adequate time for response – at least a week in the client's hands.

Provide adequate time for the analysis of the responses before the programming squatters.

Understand that the responses must be tested through personal interviews.

Translate the data into the graphic wall display.

Value

They can canvass many people in a very short time.

They can provide a cross section of information—a broad sample from different groups.

They work best for gathering quantitative information—less well for qualitative information.

They can be used to establish individual "contracts" with respondents – the individual responses become agreements for future use by the client's facility manager.

They educate a broad group of users about the project.

They prepare the user group for the interactive interviews.

Problems

Poorly designed questionnaires can alienate the client.

The questionnaire can be misunderstood as the sum total of the programming effort.

Poorly administered (insufficient time) questionnaires can aggravate the users.

Insufficient time for processing the responses can result in poor squatters preparation.

The sheer magnitude of the number of returned questionnaires can overwhelm the programming team.

Some information can best be gathered during the interactive interviews.

Summary

Keep it short, simple, direct, and easy to use. The quality of the response is inversely proportional to the length of the questionnaire.

Be sure to explain the **context** for the use of the questionnaire—that it is only part of the full programming activities.

Use many examples of filled-in responses to prime the pump and to illustrate the type of information sought.

Do not ask for an encyclopaedia—the client users will feel they are being asked to do the architect's job.

Target the people and the type of data required—people high up in the organization are less likely to respond to a questionnaire.

Interviews

There should be a clear distinction between interviews for data gathering and work sessions for summaries and decision making. Data is gathered as a basis for analysis, calculation, discussion and decision; and after having its implications determined, it becomes useful information.

No procedural distinction is made between quantitative factual data and data on qualitative ideas. In programming it is difficult to isolate facts and ideas; they depend on each other. The separate classification is made only for the purpose of analysis. However, it should be obvious that the collection of such factual data as demographic statistics, maps, surveys, traffic studies, codes, and climatological data does not require the interview technique described in this section.

Pre-Planning

The programmer should not approach the interviews empty-handed. He can identify conflicting issues which need to be reconciled. He can prepare graphic presentations leading to the impartial allocation of space and to sound decisions.

An important aspect of pre-planning is the identification of data that needs to be gathered through the interview technique. The information index is not only a key-word checklist of questions, but also the format for the classification of responses.

The client need not be aware of the information index, nor should the interview be overly structured. The obvious use of a checklist inhibits responses.

In arranging for appointments, it is best to let the people to be interviewed know ahead of time what is to be discussed. This allows them time to prepare and to collect pertinent information and material they wish to discuss.

A series of interviews is best scheduled by the client/manager, who may have to arrange not only the best appointment time for various individuals, but he may also have to arrange for work substitutes for those individuals.

The Participants

Interviewing techniques vary with the number and type of participants. Therefore, it would be well to consider four generalized categories:
1. Individual interviews
2. All group interviews
3. Medium group interviews
4. Large group interviews

A. Individual interviews involve essentially two people: the interviewer and the client respondent (C). The interviewer asks the questions and records the answers. The recording function is the most likely to suffer

A tape recorder may be used, but there is a chance that it might intimidate either the respondent who is reluctant to make commitments or the interviewer who is insecure in his technique.

Journalists are specialists at asking questions and recording them. But still, most people are afraid of being misquoted.

B. It takes two people to conduct a good interview: one to ask questions, another to record (R) the answers.

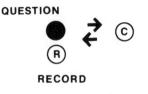

QUESTION

RECORD

This frees the interviewer from having to record and allows him to pursue his quest for information with more spontaneity.

C. Small group interviews usually involve a client leader in a discipline accompanied by one or two assistants or resource people. For all intents and purposes, the interaction between interviewer and leader has all the characteristics of the individual interview.

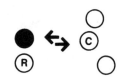

D. A series of small group interviews might well include the presence of a client coordinator (CC) who monitors the interview.

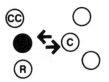

There are many advantages to having a monitor, such as checking the integrity of the answers, gaining valuable insight into opposing points of view, and providing follow-through action some interviews might generate. The main disadvantage might be the intimidation of the respondent.

E. Medium group interviews introduce the possibility of single or multi-discipline groups. A group of six to ten people within the same discipline will most likely have a designated leader who will provide most of the answers.

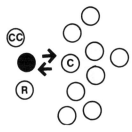

Nevertheless, the democratic process will provide the opportunity for different points of view. Medium groups require a fairly elaborate initial presentation to serve as background for the questions to be asked. The presentation might go as far as identifying the issues which must be reconciled or alternatives which call for decisions. These might be used as a frame of reference for the type and pertinence of the data sought.

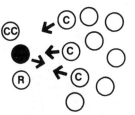

F. When a medium group involves several disciplines or sub-groups, members of each discipline might rally behind a leader.

The multidiscipline aspects emphasize the need for a clear initial presentation or a frame of reference so that each discipline can express itself on the same issues before launching new ones.

G. Large group interviews involving fifteen or twenty people may be single or multi-disciplinary in composition.

With these large numbers only half of them are likely to participate actively and then only through the motivation provided by the interviewer.

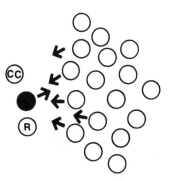

A single discipline group would very likely be headed by a leader. This group might have met previously to discuss the major issues involved in the project.

Large group interviews require an initial presentation which will inform everyone on the background of the project and the framework for the type of data sought.

The programming squatters brings together the

client team and the programming team, including special consultants, so that all are aware of decisions regarding the allocation of space and money and the consensus on quality—made within a balanced budget.

Graphic analysis cards and "brown" sheets are used as working tools to determine the space program and to balance the budget. This explicit and open process leads to a clear understanding of the project, first by the client and later by the designer.

Guidelines for the Preparation of "Brown Sheets"

Objectives

Brown sheets graphically indicate space needs which have been derived from project goals, facts and concepts. They are intended to project the magnitude of numbers and sizes. A client and a designer can visualize the number and sizes of spaces more easily if they are indicated graphically and to scale. Brown sheets serve well as a graphic technique for comparative analysis of the projects area requirements. One glance can tell where the major allocations of area have been made, the predominance of small spaces requiring a higher percentage of circulation spaces, or the unjustified equal size of different functional areas.

The first purpose of brown sheets is to present the area requirements as determined during the interviews or by some predetermined formula for the impartial allocation of space. Only net assigned areas are shown; however, the client is informed that unless an assigned area is shown on the brown sheets, it is not considered as an area requirement. This is intended to check and recheck all net area requirements.

The second purpose of brown sheets is to serve as work sheets during work sessions. For that purpose they are made of informal materials that not only lend themselves to revision, but even invite revision. (Computer made brown sheets lack this quality.) The feedback to the users starts with the statement, "These are the area requirements you have indicated to us". The confirmation starts with the question, "Are these correct"? And if work sessions on the balancing of the budget indicate reallocations, changes, additions and subtractions, the brown sheets must be revised on the spot: adding notes, changing figures and adding or deleting the scaled squares representing areas. The brown sheets displayed on a wall are used to represent the latest revisions and the latest total tally at all times.

LEARNING CENTER
CENTRAL, WASHINGTON

AUG. 1976

AREA REQUIREMENTS

NET AREA

CLASSROOM AREA

20,750

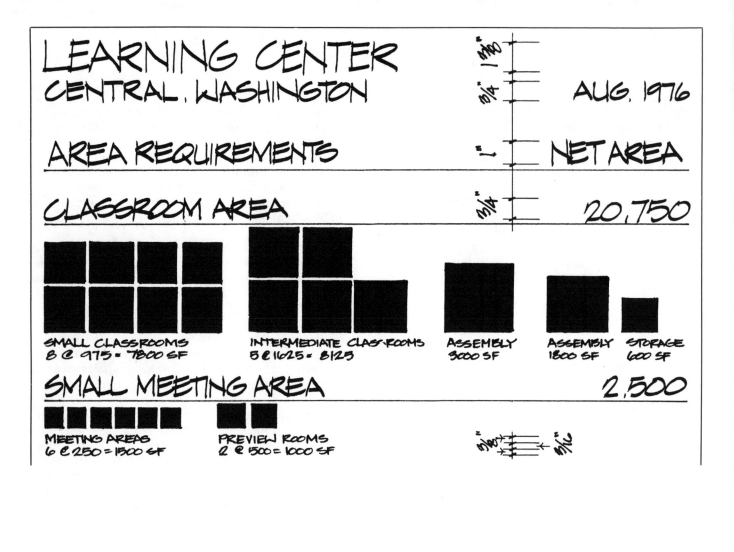

SMALL CLASSROOMS
8 @ 975 = 7800 SF

INTERMEDIATE CLASSROOMS
5 @ 1625 = 8125

ASSEMBLY
3000 SF

ASSEMBLY
1800 SF

STORAGE
600 SF

SMALL MEETING AREA

2,500

MEETING AREAS
6 @ 250 = 1500 SF

PREVIEW ROOMS
2 @ 500 = 1000 SF

GRAND TOTAL NET

72,230

60/40 EFFICIENCY RATIO
GRAND TOTAL GROSS

120,400

Time and again, the brown sheets have proven to be excellent communication devices. Not as much can be accomplished working with a typewritten list of spaces, no matter how detailed, because changes and revisions made over a period of several days on a master copy are not as readily available as on a set of brown sheets. The total scope of a project can be communicated through brown sheets to large groups of people, often representing diverse disciplines and agencies.

Dimensions

Brown sheets are sized to a format suitable for viewing by groups of 10 to 20 people. Therefore, facility titles, area figures and the white area squares must be clearly visible. On the other hand, notes and descriptions need be read at close range only by small groups of people or by the architect presenting the sheets. Specific dimensions (36" x 53") are determined by the requirements for photographic reduction to an 8½" x 11" report format.

Refer to the accompanying suggested layout for typical title and final sheets. Note that the white squares are represented as black squares in the illustration.

Informational Content

1. **Main Titles**. The project name (letter height 1⅜"), location (¾") and date (¾") are documented on the title sheet, along with category headings (1") such as "Area Requirement" and "Total Net Area". (To convert from inches to centimeters use 1" = 2.5 cm approximately).

2. **Subtitles.**(¾") Each major functional group of the facility should be listed along with a net area figure. For example, auditorium — 9,250 sq. ft., library — 11,925 sq. ft., administration — 6,785 sq. ft.

3. **Net Area.**(¾") Directly related to subtitles are the assigned net areas. More than one column of net areas are necessary if areas for future phases need to be included.

4. **Subareas.**(⅜") Under each subtitle is a breakdown of subareas. For example, seating area, lobby, tickets, coatroom, concessions, stage, dressing, shop and storage could be subareas for an auditorium. A brief description accompanies each subarea. For example, 4 classrooms @ 750 sq. ft. (30 SS/ 25 sq. ft.). Each unit area is represented graphically by white paper squares measured at a scale of 1/16" = 1'-0" or .5 cm = 1 M. It must be explained to the client that the squares are only an abstract representation of the area requirement and not a physical design shape nor even a room as such. No detailed content is included in the areas — no equipment is shown in the small squares — since the feasibility of total net area must be determined first.

One value of the brown sheets is the ability to perceive all the squares (the areas) at one glance. Therefore, the lettering of the brief descriptions must be subdued to the white squares.

ADMINISTRATION 4,225

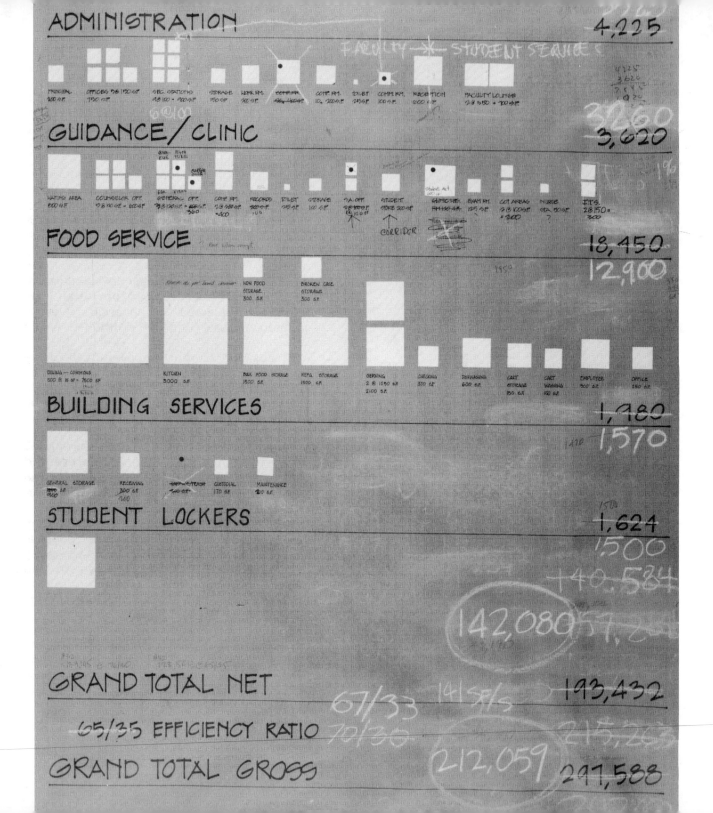

FACULTY → STUDENT SERVICE

4225
3,624
7,845
8.75

3,260

PRINCIPAL 300 SF | OFFICES 5 @ 150 SF | SEC. STATIONS 8 @ 100 = 900 SF | STORAGE 150 SF | WORK RM. 200 SF | CONF RM. 450/460 SF | CONF. RM. 10 @ 200 SF | TOILET 25 SF | COMM. RM. 100 SF | RECEPTION 600 SF | FACULTY LOUNGE 2 @ 150 = 300 SF

6 @ 100

GUIDANCE / CLINIC 3,620

WAITING AREA 200 SF | COUNSELOR OFF. 5 @ 120 SF = 600 SF | GENERAL OFF. 3 @ 120 SF = 660 SF 360 | CONF. RM. 2 @ 100 SF = 200 | RECORDS 200 SF | TOILET 25 SF | STORAGE 100 SF | SA OFF. 2 @ 100 SF | STUDENT STORE 200 SF | GUIDANCE RM 120 SF | EXAM RM 125 SF | COT AREAS 2 @ 100 SF = 200 | NURSE 5 @ 150 = 300

CORRIDOR

FOOD SERVICE 18,450
12,900

NON FOOD STORAGE 300 SF | BROKEN CASE STORAGE 300 SF

DINING — COMMONS 500 @ 15 SF = 7500 SF | KITCHEN 3000 SF | BULK FOOD STORAGE 1500 SF | REFG. STORAGE 1500 SF | SERVING 2 @ 1050 SF 2100 SF | CHECKING 300 SF | DISHWASHING 600 SF | CART STORAGE 150 SF | CART WASHING 100 SF | EMPLOYEE 500 SF | OFFICE 250 SF

BUILDING SERVICES 1,980
1,570

GENERAL STORAGE 900 | RECEIVING 300 SF 200 | CUSTODIAL 170 SF | MAINTENANCE 100 SF

STUDENT LOCKERS 1,624
1500

142,080

GRAND TOTAL NET 193,432

67/33   141 SF/s

65/35 EFFICIENCY RATIO

GRAND TOTAL GROSS 217,588

212,059

Materials

Because brown sheets are a working tool, frequently patched, cut, pasted, and reorganized, the base paper should be inexpensive yet durable. Heavy brown wrapping paper, 36" wide, is especially suitable in character and function. For lettering, wick bottles and felt-tipped pens are used. Area requirements are represented graphically by squares cut to scale from white contact paper with an adhesive backside. Self-adhesive colored dots can be used to flag special conditions or special notices.

Revisions

Corrections are easily indicated with white chalk during work sessions with a client group —keeping a running total of net areas at all times.

To modify the brown sheets, use a brown paper patch over the figure to be corrected and letter the new figure, or replace the white squares to be corrected with new appropriately sized squares.

Not all the efforts are aimed at cutting space; often space is added to the original program. But, because people can see how the spaces are organized and what sizes they are, these people can spot duplicate areas of service as well as missing areas. They can make better decisions having understood the total scope of the building, the large number and the comparative sizes of spaces. Several days of work sessions on a total program together with many different groups of people can accomplish more than years of discussion with each group separately — but only through the use of brown sheets.

After the area requirements are finalized, the sheets are corrected, photographed and reduced to a report format and for table use by the designers. The third purpose of brown sheets, then, is to become a part of the program document to be approved by the client and to become a useful design tool during the subsequent design session.

The Analysis Card Technique

The "Analysis Card" technique is a method of recording graphically information intended to be displayed, discussed, discriminated, decided upon and sometimes discarded during the programming phase of a project. This graphic communication technique is also used in the schematic design phase. Selected cards from these two phases can then become part of the presentation of the design solution for client approval.

Size and Kind

The size of a card is proportional to the frame of a 35mm slide. The standard 2x3 proportion can by expressed in a card 5½" x 8¼" or in any other convenient and proportional size. The face of the card has an almost imperceptible, non-photo blue grid based on .5 cm. The grid is helpful in sketching diagrams, charts and even in lettering. However, a plain white face is all that is required. The card is made of 100 pound pasted Bristol stock.

Working Advantages

The technique provides the following working advantages during the programming process:

1. The cards are relatively small and easy to handle. They are deliberately kept small to accommodate only one thought, one idea, simply and economically stated. This should encourage a sharp focus on each card. The single thought on a single card encourages easy comprehension. To single out a clear thought and put it in clear, graphic terms is couching basic truths. The cards are small enough to force the avoidance of unnecessary detail. This helps to keep the freshness of a small sketch.

2. The cards may be used freely, sorted, grouped and sequenced. Their best use is as a wall display—tacked and grouped under the process sequence of Goals, Facts, Concepts, Needs and Problem. The visual display together with proper classification helps to make comparisons easier and to avoid duplications.

3. The cards are ideal for recording information as discussion with the client progresses during a work session. These can join other cards in the wall display.

4. Typically, interview notes and pre-programming information lead to the making of analysis cards. These are displayed and tested during the work sessions. It is a process of *feedback* and *feedforward*. "In essence, is this what you said?" "Good! We'll pass this information on to the designer at the right time".

5. A wall display of analysis cards makes it

easy to test the interrelationships among Goals, Facts, and Concepts which lead to Needs, and eventually to the Statement of the Problem.

6. A wall display of analysis cards shows in effect the progress of programming at any point in time. As committees review the cards, they can comment, make additions, and deletions.

7. A wall display of analysis cards should be seen at a glance or two to represent the first cut toward the essence of the project. (Average display: 150 cards.) Too many cards could mean that it is time to re-evaluate the display, to postpone or discard information.

8. A wall display of analysis cards can be presented to any new members of the client team coming aboard and eventually to the design team. The oral presentation can explain the coded nature of the cards, investing their brief graphic messages with potent meaning.

9. Since the cards are proportional to a 35mm slide, they may be photographed and presented to a large audience in slide form. Or, if the time is critical, they may be presented, one at a time, using an opaque projector.

10. The cards can be photocopied two to a page on regular 8½" x 11" paper. Grouped in terms of the programming steps, the photocopies can be augmented by the typed back-up data placed in an appendix.

In this plain format, the programming package can be stored for future reference.

In a more explicit format, including captions to represent the original oral explanation, the programming package can be submitted as a report for formal client approval—and it can be used by team members at later stages in the project.

The schematic design team will not need to read the report. They will use the wall display of the original analysis cards.

A design team in action must survey and check the information with hardly more than a glance.

More sophisticated packaging would depend on the large number of copies required for approval and on a specific contract requirement.

How To Draw An Analysis Card

It takes two related activities to make a good analysis card: thinking and drawing. One needs to think through his hands. The skill of drawing gives expression, precision, and clarity to one's thinking.

Here are eight pointers that lead to good analysis cards:

1. Think Your Message Through

Deal with it as if it were a telegram. Think what must be said. Reduce it to one thought.

Put it down graphically with very few elements.

Write it out with very few words.

Add color only for emphasis or for coding.

(The illustrations represent a 40% reduction of the actual card size.)

2. Use Visual Images

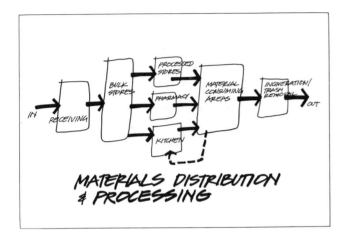

MATERIALS DISTRIBUTION & PROCESSING

Use diagrams, symbols, charts and sketches to aid communication.

Assume that a visual image is more easily retained than a verbal image.

Label the parts and give the card a title.

A flow-chart is understood more quickly than a written description.

Keep the images simple and specific for clarity, but abstract enough to evoke a range of possibilities.

Use an appropriate scale for the graphic image to project the magnitude of numbers and the implication of ideas.

Avoid minute detail as being inappropriate.

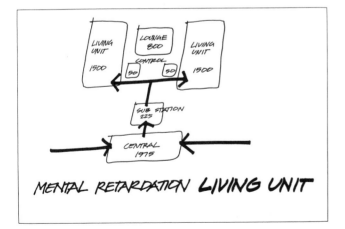

MENTAL RETARDATION LIVING UNIT

3. Use Very Few Words

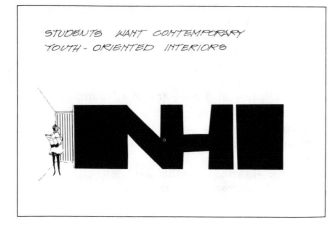

Label the drawings properly.

Reinforce the drawing with a short sentence.

State the point in as few words as possible.

Long statements impose small, difficult to read lettering on the card.

Sometimes the critical information is a number.

4. Strive For Legibility

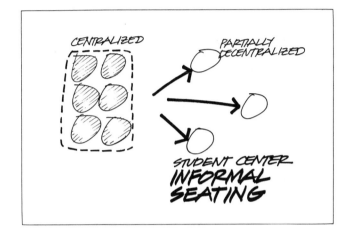

Legibility is a function of line width and letter height.

Use letters ⅛" high or larger.

Use a #2 pen or wider.

The use of an opaque projector or slides will not improve illegible lettering.

Letters on typewritten copy are usually too small and have too thin a stem width.

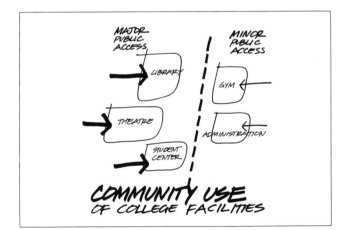

5. Design For Display

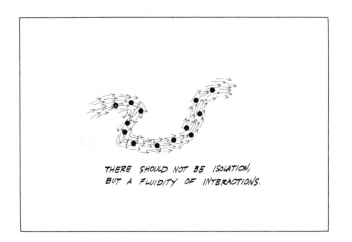

THERE SHOULD NOT BE ISOLATION,
BUT A FLUIDITY OF INTERACTIONS.

The difference between analysis cards and book illustrations is in the viewing distance.

Design analysis cards for a wall display.

There is a certain look about good analysis cards.

The bad ones are generally too bold and heavy or too delicate and light.

If you have to be wrong, be too heavy.

The two accompanying illustrations are too light for a wall display, but they are excellent book illustrations.

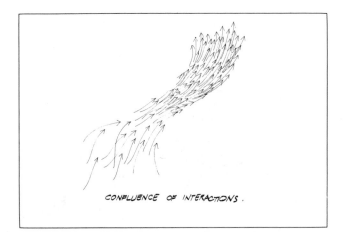

CONFLUENCE OF INTERACTIONS.

6. Plan For Cards of Different Finish

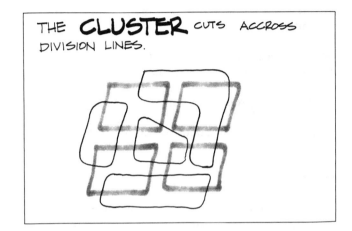

"Think" cards are done quickly by anyone who has a bit of information for consideration — using wick bottles.

"Working" cards are sketched carefully enough to clarify the thinking — using a minimum of rub-on letters and tones.

"Presentation" cards are meticulously drawn for greater precision. Assign one person to prepare the set for consistency.

All cards are process documents and as such should have an informal, loose look as opposed to final documents.

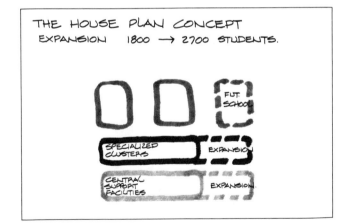

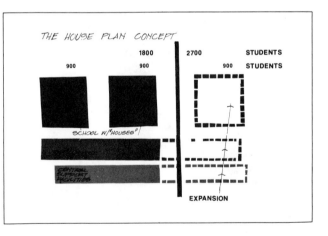

7. Encourage Documentation

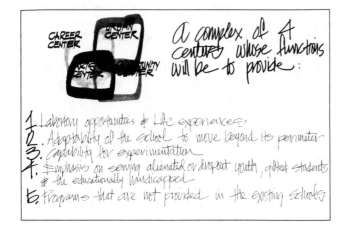

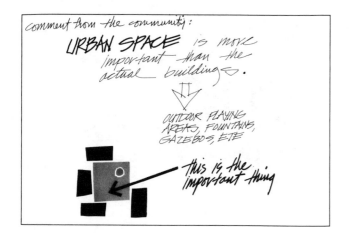

Encourage everyone on the team to produce the initial analysis cards.

Remove those inhibitions caused by the high standard of "presentation" cards.

Promote the production of "think" cards.

Be concerned with documentation first.

Evaluate and determine which cards need to be redrawn — later.

The two accompanying cards document information — too much of it. These cards need to be redrawn and simplified. The information may deserve not one but six separate cards — one thought per card.

8. Pre-Plan "Routine" Cards

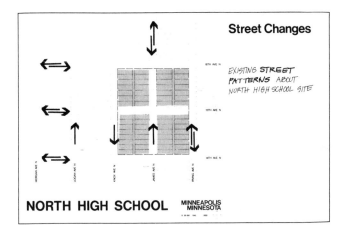

Street Changes

EXISTING STREET PATTERNS ABOUT NORTH HIGH SCHOOL SITE

NORTH HIGH SCHOOL MINNEAPOLIS MINNESOTA

Order two dozen printed base maps on analysis cards.

Document site information to be considered separately on separate cards.

Document climate data on pre-printed cards.

This is "routine" information.

If the information is not used in schematic design it will be used later. The time spent is a matter of minutes.

But if it is useful, or even a form-giver, the project has gained immeasureably.

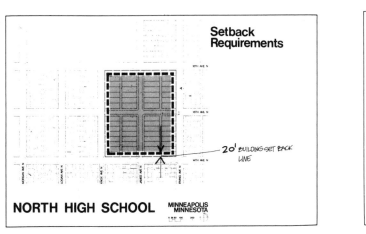

Setback Requirements

20' BUILDING SET BACK LINE

NORTH HIGH SCHOOL MINNEAPOLIS MINNESOTA

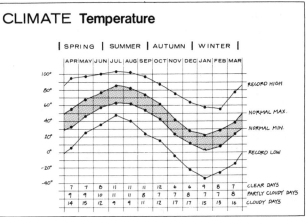

CLIMATE Temperature

Outline for Programming Reports

In 1959 (see Bibliography), we wrote: "Present the architectural analysis as you would preliminary plans." The article went on to describe the development of the analysis card technique. A formal presentation of the program is still made to the client with a wall display of analysis cards and brown sheets. Formal approval often follows. After the client has approved the program, a similar oral and graphic presentation is made to the design team.

But, more and more, the client or a funding agency requires a report for formal approval. The report could amount to no more than photocopies of the analysis cards and photo reductions of the brown sheets together with enough text to explain the total program. This could be done within a standard report outline. The report could also be a very elaborate document intended to be approved by many agencies concerned with many different levels of detail. In this case, it would be best to seek approval on a format which would make program evaluations and approvals comparatively easy for those many agencies.

Now back to a standard outline, whether for a simple or an elaborate report. In seeking approval on a useful format, it is better to have something to offer, however standard, and to modify the format as required. For simple reports, there should be no question about the value of a standard outline. The repetitive nature of the programming process favors standardization. Some people contend that a standard outline is restrictive in expressing the uniqueness of a project. They mistake *form* for *content*. The uniqueness of a project is expressed in the content of the report. However, a very detailed and specific outline *can* be confining if it is to be used for different building types. A generalized outline works best and can accommodate the different building programs—at least for a start.

A better argument against a standard outline for the report might be that the client might not find it clear and useful. But an outline based on reasonable and orderly steps has proven to be acceptable by our clients —particularly since they become familiar with the steps during the programming process. However, there may be a rare advantage in shifting the order of the steps to provide an intentional emphasis; for example, by stressing Needs at the beginning.

A standard outline based on the programming steps has the advantage of easily accommodating subject matter which is already classified according to the steps; these steps become chapters in the report. Avoiding overlapping among chapters, then, is not a problem. The problem is not so much what to include but what to leave out...and even this can be decided by the use of an appendix. The appendix should contain the bulky, statistical data and detailed information that was used to reach conclusions in the main body of the report. The location of details in the appendix tends to improve the readability of the report.

The problem statements are not written by the designer until after the program is approved. These statements, however, are presented to the client before schematic design begins.

True, there are many legitimate alternatives to the outline of a report. Consider the following standard outline. We hope your clients will find it useful.

Outline for Report

Introduction

Background

Work Performed

Participating Client Groups

Organization of Report

I. Goals

Project Goals

Mission

Goals and Objectives

Policies

Operational Goals

II. Facts

Summary of Statistical Projections

Staffing Requirements

User Description

Evaluation of Existing Facilities

Site Analysis

Urban Context

Catchment Area

Vicinity Land Use

Views From/To Site

Location

Site Size/Configuration

Accessibility

Walking Distances

Traffic Volume

Topography

Tree Cover

Buildable Areas

Existing Structures

Land Acquisition Potential

Climate Analysis

Zoning Regulations

Code Survey

Cost Parameters

Project Delivery Schedule

III. Concepts

Organizational Structure

Functional Relationships

Priorities

Narrative Functional Descriptions

Operational Concepts

IV. Needs

Space Requirements

Outdoor Space Requirements

Parking Requirements

Land Requirements

Project Phasing

Budget Analysis

Renovation Costs

New Construction Costs

V. Problem Statements

Design Problem

Operational Problem

Appendix

Detailed Statistical Data

Workload and Space Projection Methods

Existing Building Space Inventory

Departmental Evaluations

Existing Versus Planned Uses

Budget Analyses Method

Glossary

Criteria For New Automated Techniques

The predominant application of the problem seeking method is for master planning and schematic design programming. While it is applied less frequently for detailed programming or equipment listings, these functions offer a great deal of potential for automation. However, this section covers criteria for applying automated techniques to schematic design programming.

The following questions are useful for testing the suitability of automated techniques for schematic design programming. Each question responds to an attribute of problem seeking:

1. Programming involves the client in decision making.

   Will the application help the client make decisions?

The objective in programming is to reduce information (or the number of choices), not to create more. Automated techniques should not add decision requirements simply because of the ability to generate many alternatives. While automated checklists are useful for assuring comprehensiveness or tracking unresolved issues, the most useful applications for schematic design programming are those that eliminate options.

From another point of view, client decision making is not always rational, nor is it always based on clearly defined criteria. Many forces may be at work: political, economic, user values. Test the decision rules and criteria; if the decision making logic can be stated as an algorithm (or formula), there may be reason to consider computer assistance.

2. Programming is processing data for action.

   Will the application improve the interpretation of data?

Distinguish between data (factual material), information (knowledge obtained from the implications of data), and knowledge (know-how gained through experience). Do not bury the client in data. Reduce it to a meaningful, concise, comprehensible form to assist the client in making choices.

Computer output must be interpreted for communication to the client and in turn to the designer. Don't expect the client nor the designer to read tabular printouts. Summarize it. Present it graphically. Give the summary first. The detail should follow or be placed in an appendix.

3. Programming encompasses the collection and analysis of quantitative data–particularly in the steps of FACTS and NEEDS.

   Will the application improve consistency and accuracy?

Computer applications can make possible analysis which might not otherwise be feasible to perform (i.e. linear programming) and can lead to a more precise analysis than with manual methods. In combination, manual and automated techniques provide a "check and balance," such as the combined use of brown sheet displays (for communication) and spreadsheet software (for calculation).

The discipline of computerized procedures leads to more consistent reporting formats and calculating procedures. Yet care must be taken to insure accuracy of the input data and of the algorithms. Be sure that the users are aware and committed to the source of the data and to the nature of the algorithms. Checking is essential to avoid misspellings and the amplification or repetition of errors.

4. Programming often requires processing large quantities of project data.

Will the application produce useful results or will it be a number crunching exercise?

As a data processing system, the computer makes massive amounts of data more manageable. For example, demographic data can be analyzed to identify the "order of magnitude" of need. With the ability to classify and to sort, data clog can be avoided. Moreover, the data is available for more sophisticated statistical analysis than is often feasible through manual calculation.

Look at the data. Is it up-to-date? Is it complete and consistent? What restrictions does the owner place on its use? If new data is necessary, is there adequate resource to collect and process it in a timely manner? With the popular use of microcomputers, it is wise to know if the equipment or software has the capacity to process data expediently.

5. Programming is a process involving user participation.

Will the application facilitate interaction with user groups and decision makers?

For the most part, do not expect the client to sit down at the terminal with you. The computer itself is of little interest to a user group which is concerned with its needs and knowing how these needs may be met. However, as more clients become computer literate, we can expect interactive sessions at a terminal to conduct "what if" analysis, and can anticipate requests to transfer data bases for a facility manager's use.

Computer printouts do not communicate well to groups of people. Powerful communication requires exaggeration. It is often difficult to emphasize the essence when computer displays treat the output in an equal manner. However, advancements are being made in computer graphics, imaging and publishing that will provide new capabilities in the future.

6. Programming involves work sessions at the client's homebase.

Will the application overcome the logistics of travel, time and project location?

Logistic problems are gradually being reduced,

but they can't be ignored. Portable personal computers, portable printers and telephone connection to network data bases are available.

When dependent on equipment while away from the home office, seek maintenance agreements with national companies so that repairs can be made by a local agent. For international travel, make sure that registration identification accompanies the equipment to comply with customs regulations.

7. Programming is people intensive.

Will the application produce a savings in labor to offset the costs of hardware, software, training and operation?

Remember to include all the costs in calculating the economics of the potential application: data collection, data entry, systems analysis, software development, instruction manuals, user training, operation, and checking. When developing applications, a rule of thumb is that efficiencies become marginal as sophistication increases. Accept the "80-20" rule. Achieving the last 20% of the task will frequently more than double the development and operation costs.

The advent of the microcomputer and advanced applications software allows the professional to become the system operator. While this can increase the costs of training, it streamlines the effort and improves control of the product. Moreover, it challenges the professional to develop innovative and worthwhile applications.

8. Programming is done within compressed time frames.

Will the application reduce the delivery time of a product or service?

Include the time requirements for data collection, software development and user training when determining if an automated application is appropriate. Develop new systems only when time for it has been included in the project work plan. Avoid project delivery delays. Have a manual technique as back up should unforeseen difficulties emerge.

Reusing data and copying boiler plate text provides opportunities for saving time. But caution is essential to avoid misusing proprietary data and replicating meaningless text.

9. Programming encompasses the whole design problem. Only parts of the whole problem can be reduced to algorithms.

Will the application deal with a clearly defined subproblem?

Examples of subproblems in programming are operations research (optimization), math (calculation) and data base (relational data).

Often it is necessary to determine the problem boundaries before developing a procedure for collecting and processing the data. Problem seeking works best with unique, unfamiliar and complex design problems. The most efficient applications are those which substitute for repetitive calculations that are done manually.

While subproblems which are familiar and repetitive are most likely to be automated, complex subproblems make the best candidates.

For multifaceted projects in the magnitude of a million square feet and 5,000 rooms, it is judicious to use a computer program for generating requirements and cost estimates from a space-by-space inventory. For complex projects a computer program may be used for space allocation or to find difficult affinities involving, for example, 10 categories for master planning and 50 departments for schematic design.

10. Programming calls for negotiable procedures to accommodate a diversified practice.

Will the application be useful on future projects?

The determination of how generalized (or all encompassing) a system should be is a management decision. The more specific the system, the faster and cheaper it will be developed, but the less likely it will be usable on the next project. The more general the system, the longer it will take to develop and document.

With the rapid advancement of new technology, applications become obsolete in a short time. Moreover, the incompatibility of the operating systems may prohibit sharing of data or software that would otherwise make an application feasible.

11. Programming is an organized and systematic process of asking questions.

Will the application improve the ability to probe, to diagnose a situation correctly, or to retain knowledge gained from practical experience?

An indirect benefit of automated techniques is the necessity to be organized and systematic. Often this imposed discipline improves the thoroughness of the overall programming process. With planning, these techniques help make data requests more specific and desired results more explicit.

Looking to the future, advanced applications might involve "expert systems." These are automated procedures for encoding the logic of making programmatic judgments. Expert systems are useful for diagnosing a problem based on formalized question sets, and on answers learned from practice.

12. Programming is an objective and rational process.

Will the application lead to justifiable and analytical results?

The use of automated techniques in programming is not a substitute for the intuitive thinking required in design. Nor are these techniques viewed as a substitute for input by the user. Clients do not view the computer as a black box. They do not accept the output without question.

The architectural programmer is responsible for reducing data to an understandable level while maintaining a necessary audit trail as to how the analysis was derived. Higher levels of abstraction are often beyond the comprehension of many users. They desire observable statements of their requirements. The programming process strives for a defensible basis to reach a consensus on the design problem.

Evaluation Technique

What is quality evaluation?

It is the evaluation of the degree of excellence of the programming package (the product *not* the process).

Evaluation of products should be measured in terms of Function, Form, Economy and Time. The real value of process is found in the quality of the product.

Why do we need to quantify quality?

Most people like to quantify things. We ask questions such as: "What's the score?" or "What grades did you make?" A symbol such as "score" is a good way to immediately perceive a situation. For that reason, we need to quantify quality—to have a "score".

We know all the reasons why we should not quantify quality too—it's subjective, it's based on value judgment which is different in every individual. It's not scientifically accurate, and so on. Nevertheless everyone, particularly users, judges our buildings—the ultimate products of our services. That's primarily why we are interested in evaluating our own intermediate products.

Throughout the course of a project we need to check on its quality and to see if we can improve the project during the "next step". We need to know what we have after we complete the project to see if it measures up to predetermined quality goals, and to see if we can improve the "next" project.

We need to evaluate a project at every stage in the total design process—starting with programming. For now, the evaluation of the finished building is another matter—requiring a different question set.

How can we quantify quality?

There are many ways. Here is one way. The method consists of three factors:

1. Using question sets as evaluative criteria.

2. Scoring on the basis of the whole problem—not just function.

3. Arriving at a single figure called Quality Quotient which recognizes the strengths of Function, Form, Economy and Time, and the equilibrium of the four.

How are value measurements made?

The whole problem concerns the equilibrium of the forces of Function, Form, Economy and Time—the four forces that shape every product. Equally important as the equilibrium of these forces, however, is the magnitude of each force.

The magnitude of each force can be determined empirically with the following value measurement scale:

Complete Failure	1
Critically Bad	2
Far Below Acceptable	3
Poor	4
Acceptable	5
Good	6
Very Good	7
Excellent	8
Superior	9
Perfect	10

To aid in determining accurate values for each of the four forces we have developed question sets. By using the same value measurement scale to respond to individual questions covering each of the four categories, the final values can be determined more easily. The final value for each category does not necessarily have to be the numerical average of the individual question responses, but the numerical average helps to understand how the final value was determined. The area of the quadrilateral formed by the final values of the four forces yields the Quality Quotient.

For example, the illustration shows a quadrilateral formed by the following values: Function 8, Form 5, Economy 6, and Time 3. We can assume that these values represent the numerical averages of the responses to the five questions in each category. The area of the quadrilateral can be determined by the following formula:

Area = .5 (Function + Time) (Form + Economy)
     = .5 (8 + 3) (5 + 6) = 60.5

The Quality Quotient, then, is 60.5, an "Acceptable" quality.

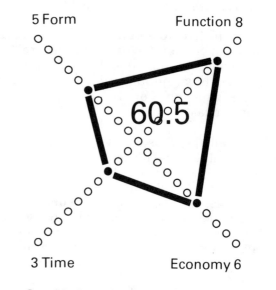

Graphic Analysis of Quality Quotient

By looking at the "score", this Quality Quotient, we can tell at a glance the quality of the product.

Values fall in the following ranges:

Not Acceptable	0-49
Acceptable	50-71
Good	72-97
Very Good	98-127
Excellent	128-161
Superior	162-199
Perfect	200-

Perfection, of course, is only theoretical. But the pursuit of perfection is absolutely necessary.

Question Sets

The only difference between the accompanying two question sets is the format. The full sentence question set is intended for those people without experience in its use. After using it several times, a person could change to the key word question set—an abbreviated form with implied wording. For example: "Organizational concept *meaning* the big functional idea". "Functional goals and relationships *meaning* convenient and efficient operations.

Full Sentence Question Set For Programming Package

Function

A. To what extent have *organizational concepts* been uncovered?

B. How well documented are the client's *functional relationships* and goals?

C. How much discrimination has been used to distinguish between important *form givers* and details?

D. How *realistic* are the *space requirements* based on statistical projections, client needs and building efficiency?

E. How well identified are the *user's characteristics* and needs?

Form

F. How clearly expressed are the client's *form goals*?

G. To what degree was *rapport* established with the client and the design team on *quality* as the cost per square foot?

H. How thoroughly is the *site* and *climate data* analyzed and documented?

I. To what extent has the *surrounding* neighborhood been analyzed for its social, historical and aesthetic implications.

J. To what extent have *psychological environment* concepts been uncovered?

Economy

K. To what extent are the client's *economic goals* and *budget limitations* defined?

L. How well documented is the *local cost data* considering methods of financing, planning and construction?

M. How well documented are the factors of climate and activities considering *maintenance* and *operation* costs?

N. How comprehensive and realistic is the *cost estimate analysis*?

O. To what extent have *economy concepts* been uncovered?

Time

P. To what extent does the program consider *historical preservation* and *cultural values*?

Q. To what degree have *major activities* been identified as *static or dynamic*?

R. To what extent does the program anticipate the effects of *change and growth*?

S. How well has the time factor been utilized to *escalate costs* and *determine phasing*?

T. How realistic is the *time schedule* for the *total project delivery*?

Key Word Question Set
For Programming Package

Function

A. *Organizational Concept*
(the big functional idea)

B. *Functional Goals and Relationships*
(convenient and efficient operations)

C. *Form Givers vs. Details*
(avoiding information clog)

D. *Realistic Space Requirements*
(statistical projections, client needs, building efficiency)

E. *Users' Characteristics and Needs*
(physical, social, emotional, mental)

Form

F. *Client's Form Goals*
(attitudes, policies, prejudices, taboos)

G. *Rapport on Quality*
(quality vs. space, quality as cost per S.F.)

H. *Site and Climate Data*
(physical, and legal analysis)

I. *Surrounding Neighborhood*
(social, historical, aesthetic implications)

J. *Psychological Environment*
(order, unity, variety, orientation, scale)

Economy

K. *Economic Goals*
(budget limitations)

L. *Local Cost Data*
(local index, labor market)

M. *Maintenance/Operation Costs*
(factors of climate and activities)

N. *Cost Estimate Analysis*
(balanced initial budget)

O. *Economy Concepts*
(multi-function, maximum effect)

Time

P. *Historical Preservation and Cultural Values*
(evaluating significance and continuity)

Q. *Static or Dynamic Activities*
(fixed and tailored or flexible and negotiable spaces)

R. *Anticipated Change and Growth*
(effects of time)

S. *Cost Escalation/Phasing*
(effects of time on cost and construction)

T. *Project Schedule*
(realistic delivery)

Evaluating Facilities

Evaluating facilities is different from facility programming. The former is feedback to design, the latter is feedforward to design. Both are needed to improve the quality of the design product.

Evaluating facilities involves a systematic assessment by an evaluation team. The objectives are twofold:

First: To detect, observe and report accurately on existing conditions and changes from the original intent as represented by the program.

Second: To modify programmatic factors and design criteria, to recommend corrective actions, and to state lessons learned for programming, designing, building, and managing buildings.

The most common application is evaluating the performance of a facility once it is occupied—a post-occupancy evaluation (POE). Then the evaluation team can consider responses from facility users. After solving the shakedown problems, and after the novelty has worn off, the first major performance evaluation should take place between six months and two years after occupancy.

Five Steps and Four Considerations

There are many evaluation methods, each suited to a particular application. Some are rigorous and strive for objectivity; others must provide expedient answers and are more subjective. This method is pragmatic – it is comprehensive, yet simplified enough for practical application.

The process has five steps:

1. Establish the **purpose**

2. Collect and analyze **quantitative** information

3. Identify and examine **qualitative** information

4. Make an **assessment**

5. State the **lessons learned**

The process is general enough to be suitable for many types of facilities. The content makes the evaluation specific. For evaluating building performance, it is important to address four major considerations:

Function

Form

Economy

Time

Like programming, evaluating involves an organized process of inquiry, which is comprehensive in content. Organization of an evaluation (feedback) corresponds to the framework used in programming (feedforward). The similarity of organization, content, and format increases the usefulness of the results.

1. Purpose

It is essential that everyone involved has a clear understanding of why the evaluation is being undertaken. An evaluation may serve many purposes.

To *justify* actions and expenditures.

To *measure* design quality (conformance to requirements).

To *fine tune* a facility.

To *adjust* a repetitive program.

To *research* man/environment relationships.

To *test* the application of new ideas.

2. Quantitative Description

The second step, preparing a quantitative description, includes collecting factual data on the building as designed; for example, the floor plan. Analyzing parametric data provides a basis for comparing this facility with similar ones.

Functional Adequacy. A measure of the amount of area per the facility's primary unit of capacity. Example: gross area per seat in an auditorium.

Space Adequacy. Gross area of a building is the sum of the net assigned area and the unassignable area. The ratio of net assigned area to the gross building area measures the efficiency of the floor plan layout.

Construction Quality. The unit cost associated with the quality level of the building measured as the building cost per gross square feet.

Technical Adequacy. The cost of fixed and special equipment, such as stage equipment in an auditorium. Measured as a percentage of the building cost, though it is also possible to represent as a unit cost.

Energy Performance. A measure of the amount of energy per gross square foot consumed for the standard operation of a building.

User Satisfaction. Obtaining some form of a reading on how satisfied users are with the facility.

3. Qualitative Description

A qualitative description includes examining the client's goals for the facility, the programmatic and design concepts for achieving those goals, and the statements representing design problems that the designer intended to solve. This step also includes identifying changes that have taken place since occupancy, and current issues confronting the occupants and owner.

Goals convey the client's stated intentions. Sometimes clients express great aspirations that are not fully achievable in the end.

Concepts are ideas for realizing goals. Programming concepts represent abstract relationships and functional arrangements. Design concepts are physical responses that provide a unifying theme to the solution.

Problem statements represent a recognition of the critical project conditions, and a direction for the design effort.

Changes since occupancy are indicators of new requirements, or inadequacies. Changes are actions taken to alleviate undesirable conditions.

Issues are unsettled and controversial decisions that are in dispute. They are posed by the occupants or owner of the facility, or raised by the evaluation team.

4. Assessment

The assessment requires interpretation and judgement by an evaluation team. This team should represent different points of view, and have a unique set of experiences, prejudices and expertise. The collection of these diverse judgements leads to a more objective evaluation.

A team might encompass the following roles:

1. Owner

2. Facilities Manager

3. User Representative

4. Programmer

5. Designer

6. Project Manager

The evaluation criteria are standard questions that reflect important values. The evaluation team should review the question set prior to reaching a judgement to understand the meaning of the criteria. Each evaluator forms a subjective response as to the *degree of excellence* attained by the facility. Refer to page 195.

A comprehensive evaluation concerns the equilibrium of all the forces that shaped the project, and is represented by a quality quotient (QQ). Refer to page 188 for the equation which yields this quality quotient.

Quality is a value judgment that varies with every individual. It is subjective. Nonetheless, quantification is useful.

First, rating provides a mechanism for identifying the *differences in perception* of a building by the various evaluators. Better understanding is possible when the evaluation team discusses these differences.

Second, rating provides an *explicit pattern* of how the parts contribute to the whole assessment. Clearer knowledge of the strengths and weaknesses is possible when the evaluators compare these patterns and discuss them.

5. Lessons Learned

Lessons learned are conclusions about *strengths* or *weaknesses*. Rarely should an evaluation conclude with more than twelve statements. At a minimum, four statements will cover each of the major considerations: function, form, economy and time.

Key Word Question Set For Evaluating Facilities

Function

A. *Response to the Major Task*
(Intended prime function)

B. *The Overall Organizational Idea*
(The big functional concept)

C. *Effective Arrangement of Spaces*
(Functional activities and relationships)

D. *Exciting and Efficient Circulation of People and/or Things*
(flow, orientation, kinesthetic experience)

E. *Provision of an Appropriate Amount of Space*
(programmed, unprogrammed)

F. *Response to User Physical Needs*
(comfort, safety, convenience, privacy)

G. *Response to User Social Needs*
(health, interaction, sense of community)

Form

A. *Creativity and Excellence in Design*
(imagination, innovation, ingenuity)

B. *A Strong, Clear Statement of Total-Form*
(plastic, planer, skeletal form)

C. *Response to the Nature of the Site*
(physical, historical, aesthetic)

D. *Provisions for Psychological Well Being*
(order, unity, variety, color, scale)

E. *Integration or Expression of Systems*
(structural, mechanical, electrical)

F. *Design Excellence of Connections*
(ground, sky, and details)

G. *Symbolism of a Generic Nature*
(appropriate expression, character)

Economy

A. *Appropriate Simplicity or Complexity*
(clarity or ambiguity)

B. *Ease of Maintenance and Operation*
(response of materials and connections to climate and activities)

C. *Most for the Money*
(good return for investment)

D. *Realistic Solution to a Balanced Budget*
(cost control)

E. *Maximum Effect with Minimum Means*
(elegance, efficiency)

F. *Lean/Clean or Rich Elaboration*
(machine aesthetics or ornamentalism)

G. *Energy Conservation*
(energy efficient)

Time

A. *Use of Materials and Technology of the Time*
(spirit and expression of the times)

B. *Fixed Spaces for Specific Activities*
(major static activities)

C. *Convertible Spaces for Changes in Function*
(dynamic activities)

D. *Provision for Growth*
(expansibility)

E. *Vitality and Validity over Time*
(sustaining quality)

F. *Historical and Cultural Values*
(significance, continuity, familiarity)

G. *Advanced Materials and Technology*
(new forms, supportive tools)

Function

When evaluating functional performance, refer to the original goals and concepts of the program. The original program provides an immediate focus on the important client decisions that influenced the design.

Form

The evaluation must include aesthetic standards to determine the physical design excellence of the building. This is the most difficult part of the evaluation, since aesthetic standards are ever-changing.

Economy

It is important to consider the original quality level of the facility–the quality commensurate with the initial budget. It is unrealistic to wish for a grand quality if the original budget allowed for no more than an economical level.

Time

Because two or three years may elapse between programming and occupancy, the initial users may be different from those involved in the initial planning. A certain amount of user satisfaction, therefore, depends on periodic interior design, or on the degree that partition and utility service changes are possible within the basic structure.

Evaluation Activities

The typical sequence of activities:

1. Initiation–This meeting is to establish the purpose of the evaluation and to identify the background data requirements.

2. Preparation–This task requires background research to prepare the quantitative and qualitative descriptions. The material is drawn on analysis cards.

3. Tour–The evaluation team makes a visual inspection of the facility. During the tour, evaluators may undertake random interviews with users and probe for responses about performance.

4. Discussion–After the tour the evaluators meet to discuss their observations.

5. Assessment–Each evaluator makes a judgment as to the facility's success by assigning a score. The ratings are recorded on a special graph, which illustrates the pattern of each assessment.

6. Summation–The evaluation team reviews the wall display and prepares a statement of the lessons learned.

7. Presentation–Using the analysis cards, the team leader presents the conclusions.

8. Documentation–The team leader prepares a report by photocopying the analysis cards.

With a trained evaluation team, it is possible to complete the evaluation procedure within a week. For a typical building evaluation, however, the duration of the procedure might last four weeks. Elaborate user satisfaction surveys may extend the duration of the preparation phase. Sophisticated reports may lengthen the documentation phase.

Conclusion

This method is practical enough for use in evaluating most facility types. The five-step process suits many purposes.

The criteria are comprehensive, encompassing four major considerations: function, form, economy and time.

The method acknowledges user satisfaction, though the final assessment requires the judgments of an evaluation team.

Six months to two years after initial occupancy is the best period for conducting a post-occupancy evaluation.

As an aid to the programming process, however, an appropriate time for conducting an evaluation is prior to initiating a new building program, remodeling, or discontinuing the use of a facility.

The results are readily usable because the formats and organization are compatible with those used in programming and schematic design.

The procedure allows for quick starts and for timely completion.

Selected Bibliography

In 1959 we wrote an article on "Architectural Analysis" based on ten years' practice of programming. We were long on practice, short on theory. Serious students of programming may be interested in the following selected bibliography which influenced the theory behind the evolving problem seeking method.

Books

Bruner, J. *The Process of Education.* Cambridge, Mass.: Harvard University Press, 1962.

Haefele, John W. *Creativity and Innovation.* New York: Reinhold Publishing Co., 1962.

Osborn, Alex F. *Applied Imagination Principles and Procedures of Creative Problem Solving.* New York, N.Y.: Scribner, 1963.

Polya, G. *How To Solve It.* Garden City, N.Y.: Doubleday Anchor, 1957.

Taylor, Irving A. "The Nature of the Creative Process." *In Creativity, An Examination of the Creative Process,* Ed. Paul Smith. New York, N.Y.: Hastings House, 1959.

Periodicals

Archer, L. Bruce. "Systematic Method for Designers." *Design,* No. 172 (April 1963), pp. 46-49.

Peña, William M. and William W. Caudill. "Architectural Analysis—Prelude to Good Design." *Architectural Record,* May 1959, pp. 178-182.

Index

Acknowledgements

CRSS Team

Editor: Roseanne Terry Elisei

Editorial Assistance: Aleen Caudill

Research Librarian: Nancy Acker Fleshman

Research Assistant: Kevin Williams
Syd Spain
Bill Campanella

Graphics: Jon Yee
Scott Carothers

Photographers: Jim Parker, pgs. 17, 57
Paola Isola, pg. 164

We are grateful to those CRSS programmers, past and present, who have contributed to this book – some much more than others – but all contributing more than they realize.